ARTISTS IN UNIFORM

ARTISTS IN UNIFORM

A STUDY OF LITERATURE AND BUREAUCRATISM

Max Eastman

OCTAGON BOOKS

A DIVISION OF FARRAR, STRAUS AND GIROUX

New York   1972

Wingate College Library

Reprinted 1972

by special arrangement with Mrs. Max Eastman

OCTAGON BOOKS

A DIVISION OF FARRAR, STRAUS & GIROUX, INC.

19 Union Square West

New York, N.Y. 10003

Library of Congress Cataloging in Publication Data

Eastman, Max, 1883-1969.
    Artists in uniform.
    Reprint of the 1934 ed.
    "Lenin's views of art and culture, by Vyacheslav Polonsky . . ."
    Translated . . . [by the author] with slight abbreviation, from Polonsky's Outline of the literary movement of the revolutionary epoch": p. 217-252.
    Includes bibliographical references.
    1. Russia—Politics and government—1917-1936. 2. Literature and state—Russia. 3. Russia—Intellectual life. 4. Communism—Russia. I. Polonskii, Viacheslav Pavlovich, 1886-1932. II. Title. III. Title: Literature and bureaucratism.
DK267.E25   1972   914.7′03′0841   72-8906
ISBN 0-374-92453-8

ARTISTS IN UNIFORM

CONTENTS

— v —

CONTENTS

PART III   ART AND THE MARXIAN PHILOSOPHY

SUPPLEMENT

INTRODUCTORY

THIS IS A SOMBRE BOOK, AND WILL BE DENOUNCED AS "counter-revolutionary" by those who think the world can be saved by Soviet ballyhoo. I do not think it can. I am on the side of the soviets and of the proletarian class struggle. But I think that critical truth-speaking is an element of that struggle essential to its success.

It is one of the peculiar traits of the political regime set up by Stalin that, instead of arguing with honest Bolshevik critics who have courage, he denounces them as counter-revolutionists and puts them in jail. This makes it difficult for their supporters outside Russia to make clear their position. If either the communist party constitution or the constitutions of the Soviet Republics were lived up to, it would be simple to state that one is loyal to the Soviet Union but opposed to the Stalin leadership. Since, however, anyone who raises a whisper in opposition to Stalin is expelled instantly from the party and branded not only throughout Russia, but in the official communist press throughout the world, as an enemy of the Soviet Union, and is indeed attacked with twice the ferocity shown to its real enemies, that simple statement seems complicated and unclear. It is, however, so far as I am concerned, a complete statement of the fact.

Socialism can not be built without science, and science demands honesty of mind. Those who understand this will not keep mute lest some frail spirits, knowing the facts about Stalinism, lose faith in the whole revolutionary effort. The future of mankind does not rest with those weaklings. It does not depend in any degree upon the keeping up of false raptures.

The efforts toward socialist construction in the Soviet Union must inevitably serve the world movement in some sense as a guide. These efforts should not be followed, however, as a seamstress follows a pattern, but as a scientist repeats an experiment, progressively correcting the errors and perfecting the successful strokes. To this end the bad features as well as the good must be confronted and defined. This book confronts two of the worst features of the Soviet experiment as it developed after Lenin died—bigotry and bureaucratism—and shows how they have functioned in the sphere of arts and letters. It is written in no utopian mood of general protest against human imperfection, but with the circumspect belief that in other countries the economic system can be revolutionized without these extreme sacrifices of what is good and of great hope in human civilization.

I have debated in my mind whether this book should be delayed, in view of the reactionary world-tendency of the moment. I have sought the advice of those whom I consider politically wise. The decision was not lightly taken.

MAX EASTMAN

PART I

THE ARTISTS' INTERNATIONAL

CHAPTER I

THE KHARKOV CONGRESS

PEOPLE ARE TAKING SIDES IN THE CURRENT DISCUSSION about art and propaganda without a full understanding of what the issue is. It is not merely the robust and socially serious attitude towards art demanded by a world in revolution which has given rise to this argument. It is a systematic effort of the bureaucratic political machine set up in Soviet Russia after Lenin died to whip all forms of human expression into line behind its organizational plans and its dictatorship. In this effort it is aided by an antiquated philosophy of the universe, which, even when liberally interpreted, is in conflict with the method and the spirit of science, but which in the hands of these bureaucrats becomes a veritable theological bludgeon with which men of independent thought and volition are subdued to silence or conformity.

Not only must all art be propaganda in Soviet Russia, whether the artist will or no, but according to the prevailing view this propaganda should be created or carried on in a systemized fashion, like any kind of commodity production or public engineering work, under the direct control and guidance of the political power. Such slogans as "the five-year plan in poetry," the "magnetostroy of art and literature," "poetic shock troops," "collective creation," "the art job," the "turning out of literary commodities," "poetry as socially responsible labor," the "creative duty to the socialist fatherland," the "militant struggle for partyism in the arts," "the seizure of power in literature," "the Bolshevik creative line"—such slogans have held the field for eight years in the Soviet Union without successful competition. The gifted poet Ilya Selvinsky shouts to his comrades:

> "Let's ponder and repair our nerves,
> And start up like any other factory."

And the amazing Tretiakov, a veritable virtuoso in the art of honestly believing all these slogans, thus sketches the future of the literary arts:

"We foresee the operation of literary workshops where the functions are divided . . . That is, the workshop will contain specialists of an extra-literary order, having valuable material at their disposal (voyages, investigations, biographies, adventures, organizational and scientific experiments); alongside them fixators will be at work gathering necessary material, happenings, notes, documents (this work is analogous to newspaper reporting). The mounting of the received materials in this or that sequence, the working up of the language in dependence upon the public for which the book is being written— this is the job of the literary formulators . . . The testing out of the social political effect—that is the work now carried out in embryonic form by our

Gublit and Glavlit . . . We can't wait forever while the professional writer tosses in his bed and gives birth to something known and useful to him alone. We assume that book production can be planned in advance like the production of textiles or steel."

Some people who love poetry in a different way from tracts, and who find this a rather disturbing prospect, will be inclined to dismiss it as one of those peculiarly "Russian" manifestations about which the regular parts of the world do not have to worry. It is true that many Russian manifestations have a quaint peculiarity. It is not a racial, but a cultural peculiarity, largely explained by Trotsky with his "law of combined development." A backward country does not pass obsequiously through all the stages of growth traversed by those which went before; it borrows traits of high development from them, and makes great leaps, and here and there even outstrips them, and in general presents a somewhat ludicrous picture (this adjective is mine, not Trotsky's) of extreme advancement and sophistication linked up with a primitive equipment and a naïve habit of mind. Russia has somewhat the mind that an awakening mediæval Europe would have had, if science and modern capitalistic culture had opened on her like a flashlight in the dark. It is very important for those who accept Russian leadership in the matter of proletarian revolution, to realize this fact. The revolution came in Russia not because Russian culture and Russian intelligence in general were in advance of that of other countries, but for the opposite reason, because Russia was a backward country, which nevertheless possessed a proletariat. Lenin, whose culture was international, took more than one occasion to remind his followers of this.

It would be a wonderful thing if some of the communists in other countries, instead of lapping up like little obedient doggies every word dropped from the lips of any Russian Bolshevik, would stand up on their hind legs and look around the world. They would see that in many respects, Russia, notwithstanding her successful revolution, is behind the intellectual standards of the other countries. The leadership even of the Bolshevik party—since Stalin threw out the internationalists and inaugurated a reign of strictly Russian, where not indeed Georgian, mediocrities in its guiding groups—is in large areas, notwithstanding the Marxian credo, a retrograde leadership. However, I do not see any signs that western communists are going to assume an erect position for some time to come—not at least until they take the voting control of the International out of the hands of the Russian party. And so, while I agree that this extreme idea of Fordizing and Taylorizing art, and producing masterpieces by word-of-order from the Politburo of a party, is a very "Russian" thing—the output of a mediæval mind surprised by the machine technique, not of a progressive mind at home within it—still I cannot quietly dismiss it with that thought. The influence of Russian ways of thinking upon the forward-going experimental portions of the human race is vast and subtly engineered, and the best artists, generally speaking, are a forward-going experimental tribe.

In November, 1930—to illustrate this point—a solemnly enthusiastic congress of artists and authors, predominantly young, and representing twenty-two countries, which is the civilized world, met in Kharkov, the capital of the Soviet Ukraine, and resolved upon the world-wide "mass organization" of art and literature as "weapons of the working class in its struggle for power." Their mood may be summed up in the words of the international secretary, Bela Illés of Hungary, who spoke in a uniform presented to him by the Red Army. Alluding to this formidable costume, he exclaimed: "Pen in hand, we are soldiers of the great invincible army of the international proletariat!" I imagine that if there had been a humorous artist present, and one with a pencil in hand, this uniformed soldier going into battle armed with a pen might have fared badly under the table. But that congress, to the best of my information about it, was distinguished by an almost total lack of mirth. In the whole two hundred and forty-six page report of its proceedings there is no single glimmer of humorous wit, not one ray of that splashing light which plays over the surface of a deliberation that is self-confident and sure of its truth. The document is speckled with parentheses reading "applause," "loud applause," "loud and prolonged applause," but the word "laughter" never once occurs. "Loud and prolonged laughter" would have been impossible, if the earth had suddenly scratched his back at Kharkov.

To those who know—and all wise men, whatever their æsthetic theory, do know—how much great art has had its root-hold in the mood of play, this fact is not a small one. For my part, I find it difficult to think that any man in full possession of his sense of humor could subscribe to all the solemn trumpery put out at once as sacred dogma and maturest science of æsthetics, by those fervently sophomoric under-secretaries of the department of "literary politics" in social-bureaucratic Russia, who completely bossed the congress. The sense of humor is close cousin to a sense of proportion, and there was no proportion in these pilgrims. They came to Russia like Mohammedans to Mecca, and they knelt fervently and received in awe the blessing of a complete communication of the sacred dogma from its ordained imams and officials.

The principles dictated to these representatives of the world's arts and letters by a juvenile lieutenant of the political bureaucracy named Auerbach, a born organizer whose writings show as much sense of the nature of creative art as you would expect to find in the complete works of Grover Whalen, may be summed up as follows. (They were dictated by this young man, and subscribed to by the world's arts and letters without one word—so far as the official report suggests—one thoughtful word of demur, question, request for elucidation, amendment, objection, reflection, meditation or intimation that the world's arts and letters possessed either a cerebral cortex or a spinal column.)

1) *Art is a class weapon.*

This Russian phrase has become the motto of the American affiliates, the John Reed Clubs, although it is the most accurate possible contradiction of the character of John Reed and everything he ever put forth as an artist. "This class struggle plays hell with your poetry," are the last words I remember from his lips.

2) Artists are to abandon "individualism" and the fear of strict "discipline" as petty bourgeois attitudes.

3) Artistic creation is to be systemized, organized, "collectivized," and carried out according to the plans of a central staff like any other soldierly work.

4) This is to be done under the "careful and yet firm guidance of the Communist Party."

5) Artists and writers of the rest of the world are to learn how to make proletarian art by studying the experience of the Soviet Union.

6) "Every proletarian artist must be a dialectical materialist. The method of creative art is the method of dialectic materialism."

7) "Proletarian literature is not necessarily created by the proletariat, it can also be created by writers from the petty bourgeoisie," and one of the chief duties of the proletarian writer is to help these non-proletarian writers "overcome their petty bourgeois character and accept the view-point of the proletariat."

This last point provoked the only discussion which suggested that the delegates were vitally interested in literary art. It seemed indeed almost their dominant aim —second only, at least, to organizing themselves, and far closer to them than the thought of writing anything, to "win over" gifted and distinguished authors from the petty bourgeoisie—what we in America call "radicals"—and "re-educate" them in all the extreme points of the proletarian program and the Marxian philosophy. They cite John Reed as a petty bourgeois writer who was thus re-educated—although this is far from true—and John Dos Passos as a promising candidate for re-education. Toward the French writer Henri Barbusse their attitude is one of desperate patience with an obtuse and unruly pupil. Barbusse insists upon solidarizing with the communist movement, and is even willing to pronounce the key-word *dialectic,* but he is about as apt or willing to understand Marxism as Al Smith. Their attitude toward Romain Rolland is what must be the attitude of earthly beings who find themselves compelled to educate the cherubim. Rolland remained "above the battle" not only of nations but of classes while the battle raged, and there is naturally some constraint mingled with the reverent joy that greets him now in the hush of an armed truce when he alights, with unstained wings and the same heavenly gestures and priestlike words about humanity and truth, amid the fighting ranks of the proletariat. Another pupil who causes these young teachers a good deal of trouble is Upton Sinclair. He has probably done more for the cause they represent than any other writer in the world, and he is a great man in Soviet Russia, but still he is obstinately chock full of "Christian socialist prejudices," and has to take his place with Barbusse and Rolland in the awkward squad of the literary infantry of the revolution. "We may make use of Sinclair's name," said an American delegate, "but we must not over-rate his revolutionary potentialities." Dreiser, Sherwood Anderson, André Gide and others have made their sharp moves leftward since this congress—partly, it is possible, as a result of its campaign to re-educate them—and their revolutionary potentialities remain at the moment undetermined.

That practically exhausts the intellectual contribution of the Kharkov congress. Its mental level is indicated in a motto provided by Stalin and hung reverently over the door: "Proletarian literature should be national in form and socialist in content"—one of those meaningless profundities like the current trick of calling social democrats "social-fascists." These phrases are meaningless until by their very destruction of meaning, their substitution of the journalist-demagog's emotion for the honest definition of fact, they become the instruments wherewith a revolutionary movement is betrayed to the enemy. The meaningless phrase "social-fascist" epitomizes the reason for Hitler's suave triumph over a revolutionary party that had just rolled up six million votes—the failure of the leadership to conceive with clarity the nature of the forces in play, its inability to distinguish allies from enemies.* And the meaningless phrase "national in form and socialist in content" tells how the zeal for an international proletarian literature is being converted into a pledge of pen-service to a Russian bureaucracy. Meaningless phrases, where clear thought is essential to

---

* As this page goes to press the "social-fascists" in Austria are leading—however belatedly—the heroic fight against fascism which Stalin's German "Bolsheviks" failed to lead.

victory, mean defeat. . . .

I am not satisfied with Trotsky's slogan of the impossibility of building socialism in one country. Socialism is a quantitative conception—it will be so even when it is achieved—and *how much* socialism can be built in one country no man knows. It is, on the other hand, quite certainly impossible to gather men around a slogan telling them what they can *not* do. Trotsky fails to see that so long as a quick revolution in western Europe was in prospect, the slogan, "We are not trying to do this alone," was affirmative and stimulated action; when that hope was gone the similar slogan, "We cannot do this alone," became a negative, depressing thing to say. Both slogans had to do, not with precise knowledge, but with an attitude to an uncertain factor. Here as on some other occasions Trotsky substitutes the logical deductions from an intellectual *schema* for that full rich human sensing of a total situation which was Lenin's magic gift. Trotsky lacks "psychology," he lacks the human sense, and those who accept him as the greatest living political thinker, absolutely impersonal in his devotion to communism, and alone in the energy and audacity of his revolutionary will, should be the most careful to remember this. By saying, "We will build all the socialism we can in one country, and the more we build the sooner our *equally vigorous effort* to foster revolution in other countries will succeed"—by saying this, which is what any simple resolute mind would say, and also is the whole of what any scientific mind can know, Trotsky could have outwitted Stalin, who was too happy to make him take his basic stand upon a negative, and therefore seemingly defeatist, proposition. The real issue between Trotsky and Stalin under this head is not whether it is possible to "build socialism" in one country, but whether the international revolution shall be damped down or led into a ditch, the Communist International turned into a Russian border police, and the Russian Communist Party become a nationalistic organization. Upon that question, to those for whom the communist society is a purpose, and not merely a metaphysical belief which justifies their taking power, Trotsky is entirely right.

I make this digression into politics—if politics can ever in these times be called digression—because I want to be free to say that Stalin, with his policy of building socialism in one country and ditching the revolution in the rest, has converted Marxism from a science of international proletarian revolution into a religion of the Holy Land. This new religion of the Holy Land is what explains the crude humiliation of arts and letters, the obsequious and almost obscene lowering of the standards of the creative mind, of which that Kharkov congress and the whole subsequent record of the International Union of Proletarian Writers—at least in its American department—forms a picture.

CHAPTER II

THE NEW AMERICAN LITERATURE

IT IS IMPOSSIBLE NOT TO MAKE OBEISANCE TO A SINCERE act of consecration to a noble end. Whether they were artists meeting at Kharkov, or dung-heavers, their readiness to pledge their skill, and if need be their lives and liberty, to the cause of communist revolution in the face of world-wide hostile armed power, would be an impressive thing. Tarassov-Radionov, another poet in uniform but one carrying a Red Army gun, counted fifty-two proletarian writers in jail in Germany alone—and that was before Hitler—and depicted like conditions in other parts of the world. Moreover this Kharkov congress was summoned with a special view to organizing a propaganda against the menace of war on the Soviet Union. In face of these facts, and our common ideal, I take off my hat to the consecration of all these artists and writers.

But consecration without manful thinking has never saved the world, and never will. To me it remains astounding that such an array of international talent gathering solemnly and pledging to make it their "life task to serve the proletariat with the weapon of their art," should never once raise the question what that weapon is, how it differs from education, agitation, propaganda— things already organized in other departments under the "careful yet firm guidance of the Communist Party"—or in what particular way or ways this supplementary weapon is to be loaded, primed and brought into action on the field of battle. And yet it is a fact that in the official record of their deliberations the sole word spoken on this all-important question is that cryptic utterance of the High Priest, Auerbach, in the Resolution on Political and Creative Questions: "Every proletarian artist must be a dialectic materialist. The method of creative art is the method of dialectic materialism."

Considering that there are probably not six creative artists in the world who know what dialectic materialism is, and certainly not one who knows what the dialectic method of artistic creation is, this directive seemed to imply that these artists in uniform were going to do an amount of straight intellectual work that hardly anybody would suspect an artist—and much less a man in uniform—of seriously intending to do. The surprise was not large or important, therefore, when after a brief period of waiting for something strictly dialectic to appear, these words were revoked by the International Organization Bureau. It is one of the peculiarities of Workers' Democracy as practiced under Stalin that bureaus appointed by a world congress can revoke the fundamental resolutions adopted by that congress, especially when the bureaus are composed mainly of Russians as they always are. Thus in December, 1932, about two years after they had met and declared themselves dialectic materialists, and their creative method to be the dialectically materialistic one, the proletarian artists and writers of the world learned through a special circular from their appointed "bureau," that they are not dialectic materialists after all, at least not necessarily so, and that their resolution adopting the dialectically materialistic method of artistic creation suffered from "doctrinaire abstractedness," and "said very little." They learned that the Russian Association of Proletarian Writers who had foisted that slogan upon the congress had subsequently proved incapable of giving "a simple and unambiguous answer to the question what it means." Hence the slogan is now abolished and the present creative method in proletarian art and literature as promulgated by the organization bureau of the International Association of Proletarian Writers under the "careful and yet firm guidance of the Communist Party" is "Socialist Realism." And lest the affiliated artists should make any minute error in interpreting this new instruction, or by any mischance continue to create works of proletarian art according to the dialectic method, they are supplied with a copy of the speeches of Comrade Gronsky and Comrade Huppert at the enlarged plenum of the organization bureau of the Association of Soviet Writers, explaining just what this latest "formula" demands.

"This formula," says Comrade Huppert in Circular No. 2, "chiefly means that reproduction of *truth* is demanded of the artist. Not in the sense of a photographic copy of reality which cannot see the wood for the trees, and only hereby obscures truth, but in the sense of an artistically true reproduction which shows up the leading, decisive tendencies, the essential driving factors . . . in their motion and their true development."

In other words, Socialist Realism means seeing all reality as a development toward socialism. Comrade Huppert further explains—what is evident enough—that this kind of realism is not incompatible with "Red Romanticism."

"This romanticism," he says, "has nothing to do with the reactionary romanticism of the past, the escape from reality by historically done-for classes. It means just the contrary. It expresses the unambiguous inner participation of the socialist writer in the represented incidents, his justified emotion in face of the real mass heroism of the struggle and work for socialism, his justified outlook into the real future, his 'dream' of the real communist non-class society which has not a vestige of illusion or utopia. Socialist realism demands of the writer life-truth. Revolutionary romanticism is contained in this life-truth, it is therefore nothing but a necessary side, an essential element of truly socialist realism."

And Comrade Gronsky explains—what is likewise evident—that this realism which includes romanticism also includes idealism provided the proper parties are idealized.

"Is it allowed to idealize people who lead the struggle for socialism, for the future society? It is. One should, and must, idealize them."

The circular conveying these decisions was accompanied by a letter stating that the news was "purely informatory" in character—not, that is, for publication—and that "the time has not yet come to express any definite views, whether the theoretical and political results of the Orgplenum, as they affect literature, can be transferred to the proletarian literary movement in the capitalist countries." Later on "the IURW will give the matter its consideration and communicate its views to all sections in a special circular." That the IURW *is*, or at least pretends to be, these same sections, was for the moment carelessly forgotten. But after all, what is the use keeping up that pretense in a "purely informatory" circular? The point is that these uniformed apostles of the new poetic breviary, these under-probationary lay-writers of the Holy See of the Russian revelation, were not only informed that the creative program they had adopted with "loud and prolonged applause" meant nothing, but they were also told to keep mum and hold their minds in suspense, until the College of Cardinals should have time to take up the question whether it meant nothing only in Holy Russia, or whether it meant nothing also in the profane regions where they occupy their humble prebendaries. Subsequently, whether by divine dispensation or the more potent intervention of the ecclesiarch, it was discovered in Moscow and made known to them in the outer darkness, that the stupidity of this solemn piece of gibberish is international, and the dialectic method for creating a new and ultimate epoch in the cultural history of man was revoked, rescinded and annulled.

Thus we may assume that any proletarian artists and writers who had or thought they had constructed works of art upon this erroneous formula have now destroyed them, and are proceeding according to the new and more accurately proletarian recipe of Socialist Realism, relieved with a discreet seasoning of Red Romanticism, and never too realistic to forget the propriety, and indeed the obligation to idealize the party leaders. We now know at least what art as a weapon really is, and how closely it resembles those lively and delightful stories told by our Sunday School teacher just before the serious lesson, showing how other little boys and girls have found it possible to have a great deal of fun and yet be good. And we see what an appropriate weapon this is to put in the hands of an association of creative writers who have dressed themselves up like boy scouts in a soldier's uniform and are going out to war for Communism with their pens and ink. You may be quite sure that they will each do one good deed of writing every day.

It is not known to me, except by rumor, how this most recent change of the word-of-command from Moscow has been received by the American creative cohorts, but if one may judge by their previous behavior it was received with humble thankfulness for the honor of being addressed. The American delegates came home from that congress at Kharkov proudly bearing in their hands a special "Program of Action for the United States, intended to guide every phase of our work"—as they fervently described it—and dedicated themselves in the *New Masses* to the high resolve that this great program should be "realized in life." It must be understood that these American pilgrims, although they reported to their readers that they "played a particularly responsible role" at the congress, were as a matter of fact regarded as extremely rough diamonds by the young masters of the dialectic metaphysic and the Stalinist political mechanic who controlled the show. They were, to be sure, the only delegation who ventured to object to anything—they thought the Orgburo should deal with the member organizations instead of with single celebrities in America—but they were also the only ones to receive a good sound spanking for their pains. In addition to this austere corrective upon a practical question, they were subsequently informed in a letter from the Bureau that their "theoretical backwardness" had been remarked upon at Kharkov. And so we may conclude that the "responsible role" played by them was mainly that of object lesson in the ignorance and ineptitude for "understanding Marxism" of the more remote and unhallowed portions of the globe.

A glimpse of their entirely "filial" state of mind—I borrow the term from one of their own protestations of loyal obedience to the parent organization—may be had in the *Resolution of the American Delegation* printed in the official report of the Congress. Here, aside from certain vaguely beneficent educational proposals that any radical-minded person could agree to, we find two practical suggestions for inaugurating the new era in American literature. One is that a lot of writers calling themselves "agitprop troops" should dress up in blue blouses and "establish connections with the groups in the Soviet Union and Germany and *secure from them both material and guidance*." The other is that "a book of

Marxist criticism based on specific American conditions is a crying need," and that "such a book could be written *under the direction of the Secretariat of the IURW*, the forces being supplied by our organizations." *

Just what "forces" means in distinction to "direction" when it comes to writing a book, is not explained. But if we may judge by the context, it means, aside from ink, pens, paper, paper clips, erasers, etc., a corps of obedient pen-pushers dressed up in blue blouses and ready to write whatever any Russian politician tells them to.

At any rate, the minds of these delegates were so extremely "filial" that it was deemed necessary by the drill sergeant to appoint a special mentor, one of those precocious young Russians who understand English and understand everything, to take them in charge, his task being to read over and inspect all the proletarian art and literature put out by these backward representatives of an outlying hemisphere, and in a periodic report to the International explain meticulously and in complete detail just what is the matter with it and how to make it Russian and correct.

A taste of the puerile, humorless, baked-mud, political-functionary brain of the young man who thus took charge of the future of American literature, may be had in this comment from his first report on a piece of William Gropper's mature and quite inimitable humor:

"The hunger march of the jobless is depicted by Gropper as a purely spontaneous movement; the artist fails to show how the spontaneous resentment

* Italics mine.

of the masses is conducted along the channel of an organized movement led by the Communist Party; in Gropper's drawing the whole energy of the hunger marchers is fruitlessly spent in shouting."

This first report came out in the autumn of 1931, after the poor Americans had been struggling along for almost a year trying to carry out all by themselves that "program of action intended to guide every phase of our work," and the report was similar to that which is made upon an obtuse school-boy by an irate teacher after taking down his pants. I blush to record the "whole series of serious defects" for which these trembling editors of the *New Masses* received such a dressing down as might flatten a worm into the mud, but would certainly produce a recoil in any creature possessing the rudimentary lime-deposits of a vertebrate organization. It was received by them with shouts of joy, or to quote their own statement—for exaggeration is unnecessary—"with enthusiastic approval."

They were denounced for "putting up a disgracefully poor fight" against social-fascism; for "manifestations of 'rotten liberalism' "; for "giving altogether too little attention to the struggle against fascism"; for "keeping silent about the treacherous role of a number of social-fascist idealogues who had formerly been closely connected with the magazine (Max Eastman, V. F. Calverton)"; for paying "insufficient attention to the achievements of socialist construction in the Soviet Union"; for "a poor and unsystematic fight against the war peril and the danger of intervention in the Soviet Union"; for "completely inadequate" work on "American imperialism and the countries of Latin America"; for adopting "an empirical attitude instead of rising to the level of leading generalizations" in their treatment of the labor movement; for "schematism and abstractness" in the same; for a "fetishistic approach to capitalist technique and underestimation of the consciousness and militancy of the revolutionary movement with corresponding over-estimation of the might of American capitalism"; for "insufficient politicalization"; for "absence of a sufficiently militant line"; for "theoretical backwardness (which was noted by the Kharkov Conference)"; for "altogether inadequate" coping with the task of internationalizing the theoretical and creative experience of the world revolutionary movement; for failing to discuss "the most elemental questions of principle arising in the work of the John Reed Clubs" or giving them "the least theoretical leadership." In view of these lamentable delinquencies—the report concludes—and "the general weakness of criticism in the American movement, the secretariat undertakes to continue . . . the work it started last year of working out the main problems of Marxist-Leninist criticism" for the American comrades, and also of criticizing for them "the concrete productions of present day American literature."

This thoroughgoing certificate of incompetence was

not only greeted with "enthusiastic approval" by the editors of the *New Masses,* but made by them the basis of a new drive for "mass circulation."

"The editorial board accepts the analysis of the I.U.R.W.," shouted these enthusiastic editors, and "on the basis of the resolution it calls all subscribers, sympathizers and contributors to its aid . . ."

There could be little doubt in the mind of any sane citizen, whether subscriber, sympathizer, contributor, or merely spectator of an incredible show, that these enthusiastically backward editors stood in need of the aid so appropriately invoked. Enthusiasm at its best is a poor cloak for incompetence, but enthusiasm over a detailed, itemized, rolled-out, hammered-in and nailed-down *demonstration* of your incompetence is certainly as shaky a foundation for the building of a revolutionary art and literature as its worst enemy could devise.

I know of nothing in the sad history of the dwindling dignity of the literary mind to equal this picture of political (and financial) abjection parading as leadership in the creation of a new culture. I know, at least, of only one such picture to compare with it, and that too is of the Stalinist-American combined-development design. In Davenport, Iowa, a small and provincial center, but one which has contributed several upstanding minds to our intelligentsia, a group of earnest comrades, having saved laborious pennies, brought out two numbers of a proletarian literary journal called *Left.* This journal was the sole rival of the *New Masses* in its mission to inaugurate a new epoch in American creative art and literature. And it too, of course, came within the purview of the Russian drill-sergeant, and received a dressing-down. The magazine is dead—it died repentant—and I need not quote the harrowing items of its "social-fascist" sins and blunders. Suffice it to perpetuate the noble record of its self-abasement, the apology for its inept existence breathed out toward Moscow with its dying lips.

"We have read your review of *Left No. 1,* signed by Comrade M. Helfand, with great care and we should like to take this opportunity to answer it, point by point, to show how the second number of *Left* has corrected the larger portion of the errors of the first number. . . .

"1. We accept and admit your criticism of the incompleteness and abstractness of the editorial contained in *Left No. 1.* In explanation we can only restate our admission contained in our first letter to you: that at the time of bringing out the first number we were . . . not sufficiently *en rapport* with the various branches of the revolutionary movement. At the present time this last has been remedied to a large extent. . . .

"2. We accept and recognize your criticism of our error in publishing the extract 'Gorky and Lenin' from Alexander Kaun's *Life of Gorky.* Please note that the second number of the *Left* does not contain a second chapter from the book as announced in No. 1.

"3. In a previous letter to the IURW we have acknowledged our mistake in publishing *French Letters, Left Face,* by Harold Salemson. In view to exposing the many fallacies in Mr. Salemson's article we have written to Comrade Louis Aragon, asking for an article which will definitely refute Mr. Salemson's and give a true estimate of revolutionary literature in France.

"4. In regard to Mr. Calverton: In our previous letter to the IURW we stated that we were entirely severing our connections with him. His name is no longer listed among our editors and there are no contributions by him or received through him in No. 2. . . .

"We confess that the Left, as characterized by its first number, is possibly an excellent example of a social-fascist attempt to win over a revolutionary trend and nullify it, i.e., that the insinuation of Calverton, Kaun et al. in the *Left* is an example of such an attempt.

"But upon this we insist: that our intention from the first has been to provide an organ for genuinely revolutionary work, and that our editorial (fragmentary and unnecessarily laconic as it was) nevertheless showed a firm and sincere desire to carry out this task."

This humiliating document, perhaps the most absolute renunciation of selfhood anybody interested in creative art ever signed his name to since the abolition of the torture chamber, was welcomed by the international drill sergeant as "healthy self-criticism."

We intended to produce a revolutionary organ, but being a group of congenital imbeciles, we produced a counter-revolutionary one instead. Forgive us, and better luck next time!

It might seem inappropriate for one sharing the hope of a new revolutionary literature to expose, from the standpoint of mere character and manhood, what scared, piddling and belly-crawling things have so far come forth in America in its name. Justification lies in the literal morbidness of the situation and the obviousness of its remedy. It needs no profound science of the human mind to know that underneath these exaggerated acts of abnegation something serious is the matter. There is no hale force here that can affirm itself in works of art. These people are sickly and unsound; their motive is not whole; they do not think about what they are going to do, but what others have done; they do not believe in themselves; they do not believe either in science or art or in themselves. They believe in a creed, a priesthood and a Holy Land. The American masses are quite right not to trust them. No man possessing the mind and will to revolutionize America will express it by wallowing at the feet of someone who helped, or has got into a position where he seems to have helped, to revolutionize Russia. The "cultural revolution" represented by these uniformed neophytes of the drill-master priests of "Marxism-Leninism-Stalinism" is a bloodless runt. Before these young men ever become revolutionists they will have to learn to be rebels. When the time comes to change the foundations in this country there will be suffering masses of the people looking for a leader. And they will be looking for him on the level of their own eyes. They will not expect to find him kowtowing toward Moscow in a position which leaves nothing visible to the American worker but his rump.

As I said, I do not know except by rumor how the latest orders from the sacred city—the peremptory excision of a whole philosophy and methodology of art from the brains of those who had gone forth to illumine the world with a new culture by the light of it—has been received by the creative cohorts of the John Reed Club and the *New Masses*. The story runs that Michael Gold, receiving this instruction in a public restaurant, was seen by some outsider tearing his forelock and shouting: "I can't stand it any longer, I haven't been able to write a word in two years!" The story is probably inaccurate, for it is little over two years since Michael Gold was over there in Kharkov dedicating himself with "loud and prolonged applause" to the dialectic method in literary creation. But it is at least true that nobody could write a word of revolutionary literature in the state of juvenile abjection before a political drill-master revealed by the acts and utterances of the group to which he belongs. These all too "proletarian" writers, veiling under a fanatic "duty" toward the Holy Land, a praying eastward, a hasty dipping of the pen at the bidding of any ignorant whipper-snapper Stalin appoints to wield the knout over them, the feebleness of their faith in any spontaneous motion of life in their own breasts or their own country, far from building the foundations of an American revolutionary culture, are handing over the creative art of the whole period, and handing over the minds of all who will count for anything in the future generation, to men who know half as much as they do, and care half as much about the future of social life, but who have the inflexible integrity of vision and speech which makes art command attention. They are handing it to men like E. E. Cummings, whose one phrase "vicariously infantile Kingdom of Slogan"—bitter-watered as the swamp is in which it occurs—holds more true poetry of Soviet Russia than all their obsequious barking in before the doors of the temple for a solid decade has held. It is true that Soviet Russia is a vicariously infantile Kingdom of Slogan—that is one of the quaintnesses of her combined development—but there are other truths that could be seen as precisely and said as brilliantly by those who believe in the future of Soviet Russia, and of the world, if the blinders were off their eyes, and the fear of the whiplash of doctrine in the hand of the bureaucrat removed from their hearts.

PART II

A LITERARY INQUISITION

CHAPTER I

THE THREE PHASES OF SOVIET CULTURE

LET US EXAMINE THAT "EXPERIENCE OF THE SOVIET UN-
ion" by studying which these artists in uniform were told
that they could learn the proper proletarian goose-step.

So far as concerns creative culture, the experience has
had three major phases. The first, from 1917 to 1923 or 4,
was a phase of natural growth, of free spontaneous experiment, in so far as a rigid party dictatorship in politics
could sanction it, and a tendentious philosophy of the
universe be stretched to make it reasonable. The publication of active counter-revolutionary utterances was in
these years of civil war and the staggering first steps of
reconstruction, of course, strictly interdicted. Nevertheless in the midst of this supreme fighting tension, the
creative arts were far more free of pressure from the
state power, or the state philosophy, than they have been
since. Lenin felt instinctively that art is not the business
of a body organized for practical ends. Doubts have
existed on this point because Lenin never raised explicitly the problems of æsthetics. But that very fact, for
those who know his mind, dispels all doubt. If Lenin had
deemed art a weapon to be wielded by the party or the
class, he would have written fully and explicitly about it.
He ignored no weapons. I have translated, and the reader

will find it later in my book, an essay of Polonsky which describes the attitude of Lenin toward creative art. Suffice it to say here that Lenin's influential wisdom, backed up in full agreement by Leon Trotsky, determined this first phase of revolutionary Russia's groping steps in art and poetry.

The second phase begins with Lenin's death—or with the first foreshadowing flicker of his guiding flame. It begins with that intra-party conspiracy which, by means of an outpour of "all-Russian and international lying" * that makes American publicity campaigns look like a true confession, had, within six months after Lenin died, robbed Trotsky of his dominating influence. From 1924 to 1932 the "experience of the Soviet Union" in the sphere of arts and letters is an experience of the gradual crowding down and suffocating, first by systematic ostracism, then by all the forms of boycott and direct economic strangulation in the hands of a state-controlled press and industry, of every serious creative impulse which would not subordinate itself to a task described as "organizing the mind and consciousness of the working-classes and the broad toiling masses in the direction of the ultimate goal of the proletariat as reconstructor of the world and creator of the communist society." I quote from the platform of the *Napostovtzi,* the group around the journal, "At Your Post," who under the patronage of Stalin's political machine, dominated that "Russian As-

* I use this expression of Trotsky's deliberately. That the lying is deliberate, has been abundantly proven. The proof is accessible in English in Trotsky's *My Life* and the *History of the Russian Revolution,* Appendices to Vol. III, in documents translated by me in *The Real Situation in Russia,* and in my *Since Lenin Died.*

sociation of Proletarian Writers" which summoned the Kharkov Congress and dictated its program. This association, called in the Soviet language by the appropriate name of RAPP, was headed by the young adjutant of Stalin named Leopold Auerbach, whom I have mentioned as a first-class organizer, and whose literary style has that rare and generous quality that you sometimes find in a business-college sophomore studying to be publicity writer for a scenic railroad.

The theory that art is a practical organization of the mind, and particularly of the emotions—pleasing news, perhaps, for I. A. Richards—was incorporated into the constitution of this all-powerful body. It accepted for membership only those who had proven themselves "creatively and by their creations able to organize the psyche of the toiling masses in the direction of the ultimate tasks of the proletariat," and it held them subject to expulsion "in case they violate the discipline of the organization, or manifest ideological unsteadiness (either in art-works or public speeches) or transgress the proletarian ethic." With these articles in its constitution and "the seizure of power in literature" as its slogan, it gradually but substantially monopolized the field of serious publication, and by 1932 had converted Russian arts and letters, in its growing regions, into a mirthless desert waste inhabited by a few sincere fanatics and a horde of unexampled experts in bootlick, blackmail and blatherskite.

The third major phase began on April 23, 1932, when with the suddenness of the axe of Esarhaddon, Stalin clove and shattered in one blow this mighty organization, swept out all courageously protesting fragments, Auerbach included, into deep oblivion, and demanded and received obeisance from the rest in his imperial decree that henceforward "cliqueism," "left vulgarization" and "time-serving" in the fields of art and literature should cease. We are now living under this benign dispensation, which is nothing but a returning zigzag, after nine years of "cliqueism, left vulgarization and time-serving"—thanking Stalin's Pravda for the phrase—so flagrantly and rankly flourishing that the chief events in literature were silences of prose writers and suicides of poets. And the return, as usual, carries us, not only back to, but far to the right of, that simple Bolshevik good sense which prevailed under the influence of Lenin and Trotsky.

It is in one way unfortunate that I, who am undeluded by the philosophy of dialectic materialism, should write the indictment of Stalin's Decade of Devastation in the field of art. It is so easy for his henchmen to reply: "Oh well, this bourgeois does not understand Marxism." However, taking a long view, there are reasons also why the protest against a State Metaphysic and the protest against bureaucratic degeneration should be combined. This tendentious conception of "reality" and "all history," this doctrine of an esoteric kind of "dialectic thinking"—"not inborn and not bestowed with ordinary everyday consciousness," as Engels said—is but a new form of the old heavy weapon of *mysterious belief* with which all bureaucracies since history began have bewildered and beat down their critics.*

* I have postponed my discussion of the dialectic philosophy to

Lenin usually ignored this dialectic metaphysics when he talked of art. Trotsky pushed it rather unceremoniously aside, declaring that "A work of art should . . . be judged by its own law . . . The Marxian methods are not the same as the artistic." They both were wise enough instinctively to feel that a philosophy which "conceives reality" in the form of practical procedure towards a goal, can not give directives to creative art, which *perceives* reality and carries a goal within itself. "I think that an artist," Lenin wrote to Maxim Gorky, "can dip up much of value to him in any philosophy. I agree fully and unconditionally that in questions of artistic creation you should have all books in your hand, and that, deriving views of this kind both from your artistic experience and from philosophy, even the idealistic, you can arrive at conclusions which will bring enormous benefit to the workers party." A sufficient indication that Lenin sensed the depth of opposition between art and practical enterprise, between art and a philosophy which identifies "reality" with the aspect things have from the standpoint of any one such enterprise no matter how gigantic. It was by thus relaxing or "putting in its place" the dialectic metaphysic, that Lenin and Trotsky managed a wise attitude to artists and their problems.

The metaphysic in itself, however, like every other imputation of human purposes to Universal Being or to "being-as-such"—is the most appropriate bludgeon

Part III, because I think many will want to know the facts described here without going too deeply into their intellectual context. For the studious reader, however, it might be a good idea to read Part III before proceeding with this story of the Literary Inquisition.

you could possibly put in the fist of a rising bureaucracy. It naturally belongs in that fist. The artistic experience of the Soviet Union can only properly be described as a failing struggle of the creative spirit against two forms of subservience—subservience to a rapidly consolidating bureaucratic caste, and subservience to a State Religion.

CHAPTER II

THE WORKERS REACH TOWARD THE STARS

ANY JUST DISCUSSION OF ARTS AND LETTERS UNDER THE
Soviets must pay a tribute to the noble efforts of num-
berless individuals in the department of education, and
of social-minded private citizens like the poet Valery
Bruissov, to develop a proletarian literature in the sense
of wakening and cherishing new talents in the classes
liberated by the revolution. The organization of "Worker
Correspondents" by the party and soviet press, although
these correspondents are uniformed and regimented in
a manner hostile to the development of genuine art, has
nevertheless aroused thousands of workers to an active
participation in the journalistic and literary life of the
country. And that, too, so far as it goes, is a service to
literature and to mankind. The achievements of the
revolution in the sphere of elementary education have
been vast indeed. The reader should bear that in mind
throughout the following pages.

My subject is creative art, and creative art in those
deeply felt and thoughtful regions, where, if it is to
flourish, it must inevitably assert to some extent its independent rights. And my theme is that every manifestation of strong and genuine creative volition, every up-
thrust of artistic manhood, in the Soviet Union, has been

silenced, or banished, or stamped out, or whipped into line among the conscripted propaganda writers in the service of the political machine. In the process of proving this, I shall cite the example of the two or three most gifted writers, the indubitable masters, in each broad field of literary art—poetry, prose-fiction and criticism.

Let us begin, then, with the "Cosmists."

It is customary for the defenders of the "hegemony of the proletariat in literature" to dismiss any writer who happens to glance up at the moon or to remember that grass grows in the meadows, as of "peasant origin." Since almost everybody in Russia, including the proletariat, is of peasant origin—and that very directly—this formula makes it wonderfully easy to get rid of heretics, and save oneself the labor of thinking about any irregular proposition. It is one of the most subtle virtues of the dialectic metaphysics, with its identification of knowledge-of-reality with program-of-action, that a man may be "proletarian" *in reality* if he adheres to the program, whether he has much of anything to do with the proletariat or not, but if he does *not* adhere to the program, the delinquency is completely explained by pointing out that he is not *in reality* proletarian. This technique for disposing of dissenters was not thoroughly worked out until 1923 and 4, when the *Napostovtzi* (the At-Your-Postites) began to take the actual proletariat in hand. Up to that date the discussion had been lively and promising of fruit, as to whether a "proletarian literature" is one produced by proletarians, one dealing with proletarians, or one championing the cause of the proletariat.

These young bureaucrats—headed at that time by Lele-vich, for Auerbach came forward when a more flexible politician was required—soon put an end to such naïve inquiries. "A literature," they decided, "must be recog-nized as proletarian which organizes the consciousness of the reader in the direction of the ultimate goal of the communist revolution, and those literary productions which do not organize the consciousness of the reader in this direction cannot be counted as proletarian, even though the authors are workers, members of the party, etc."

It is needless to tell anybody who knows something of human nature that with the consolidation of the October victory, the number of "workers, etc.," who felt more like organizing the sun and moon and starlight in their poems than organizing the consciousness of the reader in the direction of the ultimate goal of the communist revolution, was fairly large. In Moscow this large block of natural humanity formed an association called *Kuz-nitza,* which means *forge* or *blacksmith-shop.* This was the first spontaneous organization with the goal of creat-ing a proletarian literature, and its "cosmic" or "planet-ary" tendencies—so ridiculed by the functionary critics —revealed at least a natural sense of the adventurous creative rights of art.

"We will find a new dazzling road for our planet!"
"We will plant the stars in rows, and put the moon in harness!"

This tendency of the proletarians to take possession

of the universe is of course explained by the authorized priests of proletarianism as an immaturity proper to the early and unsettled period in which it arose. "Their abstractness and a certain remoteness from concrete forms of social life, an inclination toward the 'cosmic,' 'planetary' scale, can be justified"—so the *Napostovtzi* tell us—"if you take into consideration that the enormous tasks standing before the working class on the one hand, the terrible unsteadiness of life on the other, impelled these writers to broad generalizations such as found their reflection in the whole proletarian literature of that period."

In Leningrad this first and perhaps most genuine glimpse of proletarian literature that the world has had, took even more emphatic forms. Here in the days of Lenin a group of worker poets inscribed the word "Cosmist" on their banners, and gathered a majority of the revolutionary writers of that city round a slogan declaring, in effect, that man lives not in the communist movement, but in the cosmos, that up to the limits set by his success in organizing the technique of industry, he has a right so to live, and that this life of man *liberated* by the proletariat, is the essence of a proletarian culture. I think I do not exaggerate the implications of their platform. It declared that "the poetry of the collective principle, and of the joy of labor as creation, the poetry of a technically organized world, a world subjected to the creative will of man set free from material dependence—man the cosmist—is the pulse of the proletarian culture."

That this alignment of poetry with the goal, rather than the instruments of revolution, was in accord with

Lenin's feeling about art, you may see from the essay
of Polonsky which I have translated. And if you will read
the first few pages of the Communist Manifesto, where
Marx and Engels speak of the bourgeoisie as having converted poets into its "paid wage laborers," you will see
that they too felt that poetry should be liberated by a
proletarian revolution, not lassooed and lashed to the
galleys as the "paid wage laborer" of a new class.* The
goal of course is not yet arrived at; the struggle is still
on. But you may be sure that the worker-poets of Leningrad in 1920, 21 and 22, had not forgotten that. They
were not withdrawing from the fight, nor were they de-
luding themselves that more had been achieved than had
been. They were determining the relation of their art to a

---

* Even before the revolution, and during the struggle for power, and
even in works written by avowed communists, Marx and Engels demanded no such partisan propaganda as their modern epigones demand. That is made clear in a recently published letter of Friedrich
Engels, which reads in part as follows:

". . . It was obviously necessary for you to take sides publicly in this
book, to give evidence before everybody of your conviction. This is now
done, this lies behind you, and you have no need of repeating it in the
present form. I am by no means an opponent of tendentious poetry as
such. The father of tragedy, Aeschylus, and the father of comedy, Aris-
tophanes, were both strongly tendentious poets, Dante and Cervantes no
less so. . . . But I think the tendency must spring out of the situation
and action themselves without being expressly pointed out, and the poet
is not under the necessity of putting into the reader's hand the historically future solution of the social conflicts he depicts. Moreover, under
present-day conditions, the novel appeals predominantly to readers from
bourgeois circles, that is, to circles which do not belong directly to us,
and thus even the socialist tendentious novel fulfills its calling in my
view, if, by a faithful portrayal of the real conditions it rips up the
conventional illusions which prevail about them, shakes the optimism
of the bourgeois world, makes doubts as to the eternal suitability of
the existing order inescapable, even without itself directly offering a
solution—yes, even without itself, under certain circumstances, ostensibly
taking sides."

practical enterprise of revolution. And seeing that, no matter what instrumental function it may at times ful-fill, art can not be defined and judged and wielded by the practical powers as an instrument for revolutionizing life, they placed it with the gradually arriving goal, with life revolutionized. And they were snuffed out, or flick-ered faintly for a year or more in the heavy atmosphere of paid-for Stalin propaganda, and died out—not as deserters from the struggle, but as heretics from the state philosophy and deviators from "the Bolshevik creative line," the "party line in literature," the "Marxo-Leninist æsthetics"—a thing unknown to either Marx or Lenin.

> *"Enough of the sky,*
> *And the strangeness of things!*
> *Give us more plain nails!*
> *Throw down the sky! Abandon things!*
> *Give us the earth*
> *And live men!"*

By a political putting across of such slogans—wise enough in their place in a poem—the party regulars, the safe men of Stalin, "seized the power in poetry," and the worker bards of Leningrad were made aware that they are not "cosmists" after all, but very specifically located pen-pushers, they pushing and the hand of the Politburo guiding the pen.

CHAPTER III

THE MINSTRELS SEEK BOHEMIA

WHEN IMPULSES AS ADULT AND COMPREHENDING AS THAT, rising moreover among the workers themselves, are extinguished under the incombustible gas-blanket of party machine control and paid-for propaganda, you can easily imagine what becomes of those more naïve and childlike serious capers in which the lyric spirit at its purest always did, and pray God always will, express its totally impractical exuberance. Their sad story is told briefly in the dissoluteness and the death of Sergei Yessenin. It is a fixed item of the false sophistication of Marxians— sophistication which was once naïve enough, remember, to conceive "reality" as practical "human-sensible action" *—that the tendency of artists to adopt a freely experimental, slightly vagabondish mode of life, as irrelevant as possible to social classes or any other fixed and practically regulated categories of being, is a passing incident, a symptom merely of the decomposition of the capitalist regime. It is only necessary for a Marxian to say "bourgeois Bohemia," and any unfortunate poet or other seeker for a sheer and various experience of life, is therewith chloroformed, ticketed and pinned away in a glass box, and human knowledge has no more to see or say

* See page 193.

about him. Poets, however, were minstrels—minstrels were privileged magicians—before bourgeois society ever struck a tap-root into the earth. They will be so when bourgeois society, desperately practical in its decadence, has carried the desperately practical sophistication of these Marxians with it, as properly belonging to it, into the remote horizons of history. Therefore let us approach the "café period" of Russian post-revolutionary poetry, and the sad bloom and drooping of Yessenin with a little psychological common-sense.

That an artist, no matter how serious, is and in some sense must be a child, is obvious from his preoccupation with the mere colors of the things he handles. And it was quite inevitable that, with the achievement of the long-awaited social revolution in Russia, the beginning of a new era for the race of man—indeed before the last shot was fired or the new era quite begun—a veritable horde of these excited children should come flocking into Moscow and Leningrad, each with his solemn-sure idea of what the art and poetry of this new era was to be. They opened a "Stall of Pegasus," they opened several stalls of Pegasus, where they could drink tea and wine and munch a few baked crackers, and talk all night about art and poetry. They formed a poets' union, they gave all-night poetical concerts, they recited their poems along the boulevard, inscribed them on fences and monastery walls, and in general enlivened the scenery with more fantastic ideas and more "schools" of art, than this dull world had ever seen before in all its history. I was told in 1922 by one of these winged arrivals from the south, the president and sole member of the "hobo school," that there were already 40,000 poets in Russia only five years after the revolution, and that in another five years poetry would infect and conquer the whole population.

Among these schools the "imagists" were the most interesting—perhaps mainly because Sergei Yessenin, for company's sake, called himself an imagist. They professed to be a vast advance upon the futurists, a leftward movement. "The academicism of the futurist dogmatics sticks like cotton in the ears of youth," they cried. And they proposed to liberate the arts by "cleaning form of content," waging war on grammar, particularly on the verb —the "head director of the grammar orchestra"—and establishing a "dictatorship" of image over meaning. A proper poem, under this dictatorship, should read equally well forwards or back. On such foundations they announced "the first dawn of a world-wide spiritual revolution," and the inauguration of "a new, non-class, universal-human idealism of the harlequinade variety." This Russian phase of the Cult of Unintelligibility was distinguished from ours, it seems, only by a slightly better apprehension of its own inconsequence. "Thus I seize the reins of my wind-blown thoughts and fly to the nowhere in my charlatansky sharabang!" cried its extreme apostle, Shershenevich.

To the sombre Marxian critic, all this seems anti-revolutionary and a strictly "bourgeois" foolishness. There *is* of course no proletarian foolishness, for, as we have seen, proletarian reality and proletarian program-of-action are the same. To me it seems an antic of the literary mind, designed at once to get attention in a world too desperately engaged with scientific thinking and to get away from that unhappy world. I note that even the humane Polonsky classifies as "petty bourgeois" and opposed to revolution a declaration of these imagists that "joy" is the main object of their capers. And yet I find him later quoting with approval Lenin's rejection of these same capers because he "experiences no joy from them." Is joy after all a counter-revolutionary state of being?

There has always been a lack in Russian criticism of the sense for play. The black shadow of tzarism cast a gloom over their whole enterprise of culture. Even their Enlightenment had to come through the cellar in flashes from a dark-lantern. Byelinsky, Chernishevsky, Dobroliubov, Stassov, Tolstoy, Plekhanov, every great Russian critic has had but one single judgment-standard, or rather feverish obsession in his mind—"social significance." And by that they meant helping or hindering the revolution. This made a fertile soil for Marxian metaphysics to grow in and gobble everything into its program-theory of being. But it was a sad misfortune, somewhat like having hungry parents, for the creative genius of the new age. The Great Russians are not sad or tragical by nature; their own sociologist, Nicolas Seeland, was right when he classed them, according to his system, among the "sanguine" types. You could find in conversation, even in the Bolshevik party, many people capable of seeing with a humorous eye the utopian charm and quite appropriate and hopeful irrelevance of this mad flowering of "schools" of poetry. But not a word of that in books of criticism. There the proper duty is to *place* these rowdies in relation to the social and class forces, and even while they wriggle and gesticulate and shout to heaven their loyal revolutionism, argue them right back into the enemy camp.

"There can be no neutral art in a class society"—that is what must be explained in books. Every metaphor is art. And not one metaphor in Russia, not one line, or lilt, or limerick, can be innocent of "class significance." Remember that.

CHAPTER IV

YESSENIN'S SUICIDE

IT WAS IN THIS LITERARY ATMOSPHERE, INHERITED FROM the dark caves of the old underground revolt, crystallized into dogma by the Marxian metaphysics, propagated as state loyalty by the party-clique in power, that the cherubic hooligan, Sergei Yessenin—perhaps the most unconsciously melodic of all contemporary lyric voices —tried to find a minstrel's life, and tried to live and sing.

Such voices are heard only once or twice in a century. And they are the peculiar jewels of literature, not because they are more musical or moving than other poets—less so perhaps, as the flute is less than other instruments in the orchestra—but because they are the farthest away from science. They are the purest poets. Their gift and their business is all with the felt qualities of experience, with cherishing and communicating, not with altering or understanding it.

Yessenin was a rustic bard like Robert Burns who came to town and lived there with a small glory round him. His songs, like tender moonlight over rural Russia with bells ringing in the steeples, won him far too soon this place in life so different from that of which they sang. He was famous enough before the revolution to be invited to read his poems to the tzarina. She said that they were beautiful, but very sad. "So is all Russia," he answered.

Yessenin accepted the Bolshevik revolution with an immediate unreserved faith and fervor to be found in not more than six writers who had any standing to lose.

> "I accept all—just as it is I take it.
> I am ready to travel the newly broken road.
> I give my whole soul to October and May,"

he sang. And then he added:

> "Only my loved lyre I will not give."

The distinction is a fine one, and not to be found in the philosophy of dialectic materialism. Yet I think Yessenin knew exactly what he was saying. He was happy too in his decision, and in the hardships of the revolution. He says in his brief autobiography:

> "I consider the year 1919 the best time in my life. We spent a winter then in a room at a temperature of 5°.* We didn't have a log of firewood. . . . When there was no paper I printed my poems, together with Kussikov and Marienhoff, on the walls of the Strastny monastery, or merely read them aloud somewhere along the boulevard. The best admirers of our poetry were prostitutes and bandits. We had a great friendship with them."

And to this again he adds: "The communists do not

* Approximately 43° Fahrenheit.

like us through misunderstanding."

In my opinion there is a more precise truth in that remark of Yessenin about the communists, than in all the cocksure and very righteous reams that have been written by the communists about Yessenin, and about "Yesseninism." I should define Yesseninism as the resort to bandits and prostitutes, to rum-heisters and roysterers and a ribald dandy's way of life—and I must add, sadly, to Isadora Duncan in her insane decline—of a lyric poet who could not find understanding among orthodox Marxists. In saying this I do not ignore the fact that, theoretical beliefs aside, the Bolsheviks were during Yessenin's life occupied, to the point of legitimate deafness, with a gigantic practical undertaking. It is an old wisdom that "when the cannon speak the muses are silent," and a silent muse is a muse bewildered and lost for what to do. As Trotsky said in his gentle contribution to the memorial volume dedicated to Yessenin:

"Our epoch is not lyric. . . . Yessenin was intimate, tender, lyric—the revolution is public, epic, catastrophic. That is why the short life of the poet was catastrophically broken off."

It would be folly to deny the pertinence of this remark, and we should give thanks that Trotsky at least did not think the tragedy of Yessenin could be stowed away into the archives with the remark that he was a "declassed semi-kulak," a representative of the "expiring village," a poet of the "capitalist decline," the "agrarian decay," the "petty bourgeois despair"—a poet of no matter what, just so the words sound "economic." Yessenin was a representative of lyric poetry—that is, of the creative artist in his purest essence. And such an artist will not and can not in his singing subordinate himself to any kind of practical expediency, to any enterprise which has its justification in ulterior ends. The purpose of his singing is his song. And he must either sing that song as it comes up into his breast, or crowd it down and say nothing and suffer. That is what Yessenin knew instinctively and tried to tell them, tried in vain to tell them. I give my soul to the revolution—

"Only my loved lyre I will not give."

They could not hear it. Not only were they deaf with practical absorption in a task, but *theoretically* they had no ears to hear it with. Reality, they theorized, is practical human action. "All history" is class-struggle. "Social life is practical," and "the essence of man is . . . social relations." In such a system of belief the deafness of the man-of-action to the lyric poet's plea for some clear place in life, is inhumanely absolute. It was the twofold misfortune of Yessenin's lyric nature to be born into an age of gigantic concentration upon a practical undertaking, and into a company of engineers whose blue-prints took the form of metaphysical demonstrations that the universe itself, or man and all society and all history, *is* that undertaking.

The evils worked by this program-of-action parading as a knowledge of reality are not dire in the days of the struggle for power. After the power is seized and these resolute men with "Reality" safely stored in their heads in the form of a political program, begin to govern a nation and guide a civilization, then some help is needed desperately. I think this is true to some extent even of great-minded men like Lenin and Trotsky, although their frequent warnings against a "wooden," "automatic," "mechanical" or "vulgar" application of Marxism, show that they felt the peril to good sense involved in driving such a conception of reality too hard. With lesser minds, whose wisdom could not reach beyond their learning, good sense too often disappeared completely in a rabidness of metaphysical belief. And when the direct influence of Lenin and Trotsky, and such close companions-in-intelligence as Rakovsky, was removed entirely, this metaphysical belief became, as I have said, a bludgeon. To identify theoretic knowledge of reality with a program of struggle for power is a dangerous self-deception; to identify such knowledge with a program of bureaucratic boss-rule is a crime against society, science, art and education.

To all this Yessenin's story, with a thousand others, testifies. I can think of nothing more pathetic—nothing more symbolic in its pathos—than the picture of this bewildered minstrel going out and gathering in a pile of monstrous text-books and sitting down to struggle with the heavy dogmas of Hegelian-Marxian economic dialectics, trying conscientiously to become a nice time-beating preacher of the faith. The more he tried to do this, which was all that the established church and rapidly coagulating state-theology could propose that he should do, the more inevitably he fled to "prostitutes and bandits" for that sympathy and admiration which a lyric artist, to sustain his more than normal selfhood, somewhat unnaturally craves. For this also, and exactly this, he fled with Isadora Duncan on that Bacchical noctambulation through the western world. I met her just before they went, by sheerest accident, on a little railroad platform in the Caucasus. And she was full "greatness," as she always was, and made strenuous efforts—somewhat laughable efforts since she could not read the Russian—to convey to me her sense of the authentic "greatness" of this poet. She was correct in her judgment. Her poise in artistic matters was as perfect as her lack of poise in life.

Indeed Isadora Duncan's failing was that she saw life wholly as an art of gesture. Conceiving the revolution as a gesture, adhering to it in the face of all the world with glorious abandon, and yet ignoring utterly both the practical predicament and the theoretic hypotheses of the Bolsheviks, she was about as helpful to them in the reconstruction period as a small whirlwind following a hurricane. But to Yessenin, the bewildered singer, wavering between those ponderous text-books from which he learned nothing but that he was useless in the new world being born, and the drunken Moscow tavern where all sorts of friendly and loose-thinking creatures, more like the old farm animals, loved him when he fed them with his songs—to him this glorious whirlwind seemed a godsend. She gave him what he needed. One sublime gesture of her arm and rising body and those Marxians looked very small. All politics looked small, all puttering with mere actualities and problems. The revolution after all is poetry, and you, among them all—Sergei Yessenin— you are the poet.

She stimulated and restored his selfhood, but she could not steady him to any firm ambition. She was herself engaged in self-destruction. She was fleeing from her art, and from those children she had taught to dance and who were dancing now too youthfully. Her gestures were still beautiful, but they lacked that sole point of support for practicality and therefore perfect sanity in the pure artist, the purpose to succeed greatly in his art. Her success was all too sure, and it was surely in the past, and she was living her life of gestures—already with much help from alcohol—in a world no longer real. She could not deeply help or hold Yessenin. Instead of creating the great promised songs, he fought murderous battles with her in their bedroom.

He came home to Moscow from that Dyonisian demigration more than ever a boy broken in two, a hard and naughty cherub, a sweet melodic singer of the drunken sloppy perfumed sappiness of whores and sophomoric hooligans. Voronsky vividly describes his looks in this last period:

"His aspect instantly divided in two halves. Through the dudish surface of the city-street madcap, the flaneur, shone forth the simple thoughtful face of our peasant of the middle region, inclined to sorrow and gravity. And the main thing was that the one aspect seemed to emphasize the incompatibility and untruth of its combination with the other, as though someone had united them mechanically and by force, why or to what end was inunderstandable."

It does not take much intimate knowledge of Sergei Yessenin, or the ways of life, to understand this ambivalence. A sentimental lyrist with brains enough not to be mushy is always on the verge of irony, and rank cynicism is never far from him. This you can see in Heine or Byron, or in T. S. Eliot if you do not mistake him for a thinking man. These poets of sentiment, however, were allowed to lift their delicate stems of feeling into the air and give their bloom. So they kept their equilibrium. Yessenin was made to feel that his rare fragile offering was useless, was in fact an affront. His tendrils were chopped off, and he was pounded down by an organized propaganda and a practical dictatorship over opinion such as history has rarely seen. He could not turn against the revolution; he was too true. He could not defend his right to sing; he lacked the mental force. He believed what he was told by those big books and by the men in power, believed that he was useless, a rustic thing surviving like an old soft scab upon the new life being born. And with a generosity that is not too common in the lyric tribe, he gave his blessing to the newer poets who should now efface him and the memory of his songs.

He had once eagerly written:

"I want to be a singer and a citizen,
To everyone a pride and an example,
A real and not a changeling son

In the great states of the Soviet Republic."

Now he could only sadly ask:

"By what odd chance did I go shouting in my songs
That I am a friend of the people?
My poems are no longer needed here.
And I too—by your leave—I am no longer needed.
Bloom, youths, grow healthy in your bodies!
You have another life, a new refrain.
But I go on alone to the unknown country,
My rebel soul forever humbled."

On December 24, 1925, Yessenin travelled from Moscow to Leningrad, as he said "for permanent residence." Taking a cab from the station he called successively upon a number of friends, but found none of them at home, and thus arrived at the Hotel Angleterre sad and, what is still more serious, sober. He instructed the porter not to let anyone in to him, and lived there in the hotel three days. He had been haunted for a year and more by a "Black Being"—a narrowing into the concrete of that presentiment of ruin, that overhanging of an infinite despair, which had been familiar always in his songs. His verses about this Black Being have been diagnosed by psychiatrists as a very poetry of delirium tremens. He saw few other beings, at any rate, during those three days. On the 27th, wishing to write some farewell verses to a friend, and not finding ink in the room, he took a knife and cut his wrist in several places. Dipping the pen each time in his own fresh blood—as befits a sentimental poet having his last taste of sorrow—he wrote these parting lines.

> *". . . Farewell my friend,*
> *Farewell without my hand or word.*
> *Do not grieve,*
> *Do not vex your brow.*
> *It is nothing new to die,*
> *To live, of course, is not more new."*

That evening Yessenin again told the porter not to let anyone in to him, saying that he was "tired and wanted to rest." In the morning at 10:30 his friend Ustinov, who lived in the same hotel, came to his door and knocked, but there was no answer. He summoned the hotel clerk and they opened the door. Yessenin's body hung swaying in the corner, attached to the steampipe by a rope taken from his trunk. On his left arm were some scratches, and on his right above the elbow a deep wound made with the blade of his razor. He had had some trouble making himself die. The room was in complete disorder—clothes thrown everywhere—and sheets of torn manuscript littered the floor. Physicians decided that Yessenin had hung dead since dark.

CHAPTER V

THE SUICIDE OF SEVERAL POETS

YESSENIN'S NAME HAS BEEN MADE A SYMBOL BY THE BOL-sheviks for any sign of disheartenment, or loss of ardor among the youth in the great task of building socialism —especially such loss of ardor as resorts to drunkenness or sexual debauchery in the border-lands between Bohemia and the underworld. Important conferences of party chiefs have been dedicated to "Yesseninism," and many resounding speeches made and learned dissertations published on the subject. The word is firmly fixed in the new Soviet language. In the *Literary Encyclopedia,* a considerable space is devoted to its meaning, and here the suicide of poets plays the major role. After mentioning erotic aberrations as one marked element in the meaning of Yesseninism, the learned work continues: "Yesseninism expressed itself still more sharply in the suicides which removed several poets from our literature." And lest the reader should attribute a political, or perhaps even a "proletarian," cause to this unusual epidemic, it quickly adds: "The majority of them were of peasant origin, were not engaged in any social work, and found in the poems of Yessenin support and justification for the development of individualistic experiences within themselves."

Of this "majority" who so sinned against the church as to be of "peasant origin" and not engaged in "social work," and therefore of course quite properly destroyed themselves, I have no record. The two I know about besides Yessenin were not of that iniquitous nature at all. One of them was wholly proletarian, the other of the Bolshevik intelligentsia. The happy melodist, Kuznetsov, composer of intimate lyric pictures of the workers' life, was the son of a weaver and himself went to work in a factory at the age of fifteen. He was a member of the Communist Youth organization and in all ways that a poet could be, a faithful proletarian Bolshevik. "He wrote joyful verses," Voronsky tells us, "about the factory, the radio tower, built during the hungry years, and then suddenly ended his life. We could not tell from his verses that the poet was living through an inner crisis. Only after his death did it become known that he had one or two poems reflecting the mood which brought him to the noose."

When it comes to explaining an epidemic of suicides among poets as a part of the giving way of an agrarian before an industrial civilization, any sober man, I think, must see how fatally the Marxian way of "conceiving the world" can depart from the simple realities of the world. "The truth is always concrete," as Lenin loved to remember. And the concrete truth about this matter is no doubt told better in the words spoken at Yessenin's grave-side by a fellow poet, Kirillov, than in all the abstract palaver of the ecclesiologues.

"Comrades, let us promise over this fresh grave that we will alter certain adverse features of our life, and with a common effort create that friendly comradely atmosphere which will make impossible such deaths as that of Yessenin."

It lay, unfortunately, not in the power of Kirillov and his comrades to alter those adverse features or create that atmosphere.

CHAPTER VI

MAIAKOVSKY'S SUICIDE

MAIAKOVSKY'S SUICIDE IS IN ONE WAY MORE SYMBOLIC than Kuznetzov's of the state of arts and letters under Stalin. For Maiakovsky was not only engaged in "social work" under the direction of the party, but also in a very lusty shouting that such work is what it means to be a poet. "The poet is not he who goes around like a curly lamb and bleats on lyric love themes, but the poet is he who in our ruthless class struggle turns over his pen into the arsenal of weapons of the proletariat, who is not afraid of any dirty work, any theme about revolution, about the building of a people's industry, and will write agitation-pieces on any economic question." Such were Vladimir Maiakovsky's "poetics" when he died.

Maiakovsky was a mighty and big-striding animal—physically more like a trained-down prize-fighter than a poet—and with a bold shout and dominating wit and nerves of leather. I knew Maiakovsky and enjoyed him both as circus-lecturer—probably the loudest and least modulated thing and nearest to the banging in of a cyclone that poetry ever produced—and also as a most amiably gracious host. If poets may be compared to flowering plants, Maiakovsky was a great standing coarse-stemmed swamp-watered weed.

I remember how much I liked him, and yet felt that there was a lack in his magnetic presence which I first expressed by saying that he seemed in some way like a horse. I later realized that he had a rather long face and no smile. Maiakovsky could laugh or look solemn, and he was gracious and civilized in the manipulation of these and various other expressions, but he could not smile. He could not grow into a laugh or pause on the edge of a solemn expression. This lack of subtle modulation, lack of the fine shades of humor, in a man possessed of boisterous and yet good-natured wit, has much to do with the character of his poetry, which is a sincere, startling, compelling and yet not genial lion's roar of revolution and futurism. It is the biggest thing in Slavic poetry of this epoch, and the farthest thing perhaps in all poetry of all epochs from that delicate putting forth of tendrils with a view to timid bloom which poetry sometimes is, and is usually assumed to be. Maiakovsky was as robust and rank and avid of the strong blows of life as George Chapman.

He too came straight over to the Bolshevik revolution, bringing all his "futuristic" apparatus with him—the verbal circus work, the rhythmic and grammatic flying bars and colored paper hoops, and his intemperate imagination somersaulting through them—sometimes very flimsy, sometimes hardy and sublime. He declared futurism to be the poetry of the new epoch, and so far succeeded in convincing people that it was, as to get his group placed in charge of the department of plastic arts of the Commissariat of Education, and himself recognized as unofficial leader of the poetry of the proletariat. Here he was, of course, being a great blatant poet of his own personality, a ridiculous failure—somewhat less ridiculous, perhaps, than those Marxists who explain it on the ground of survivals in him of a "bourgeois ideology." There were survivals of that in everybody. The obvious fact that Maiakovsky failed as a leader of the proletarian culture because he was a momentous poet, and momentous poets are not institutions for cherishing other people's poetry, is another simple element of reality that can hardly sift through that conception of it which occupies the points of ingress to the brain of the dialectic materialist.

Maiakovsky was made to understand, at any rate, that his proposal to "pitch Pushkin out of the ship of contemporaneity," to "have the classic generals shot at dawn," and in general to go the very limit with all change, was not Marxism. It is a main point in the genuine Marxian wisdom to see one thing evolving out of another, and not become overheated even where this process takes a jump. Revolution is merely the technique of evolution. Moreover proletarian poetry is poetry which "organises the reader's psyche in the direction of the communist tasks of the proletariat," and these tasks just now do not require a new language, or a new "orchestration"—especially one which nobody can understand—they require a little pellucid plain speaking in the very language of Pushkin. So Maiakovsky yielded his place as organizer of the proletarian psyche to A. A. Bogdanov, who continued to make hash of the job, although for the opposite reason—that he was *not* a poet and could not make out what a poet is. A vast amount of ink was spilled about this Proletcult, whether it should be organized under the political state as a bureau of the department of education, or independently as a distinct element of the proletarian movement like the trade unions. Bogdanov wanted it distinct; Lenin insisted it should be an element of popular education. It never occurred to anybody, I think, that it ought not to be organized at all, that so far as artistic culture can be organized it is *nothing but* education. That, however, is what time demonstrated. The Proletcult never amounted to anything either way.

Maiakovsky, however, did amount to something. Stripped of his epaulettes as the classic general to replace Pushkin, he tossed about somewhat vaguely for a year or so, not knowing how to find in this strange "Marxian" set-up the eminence which he knew belonged to him. He finally found it by organizing his own small proletcult, independent and distinctive, without so much as a by-your-leave from anybody. He called it the Left Front of the Arts, a name which he abbreviated in a futuristical manner with the syllable *Lef*. I do not know what this syllable conveys poetically to a Russian; to me it suggests the word for *left* and also the word for *lion*, and I get an image of Maiakovsky throwing his head back and roaring loudly on the extreme left, while all the "curly lambs" turn pale and crowd over to the right in the vicinity of the official sheepfold of the Proletcult. This roaring lion, however—and here the sad story begins—humbly agreed to "direct all his creative activity to organizing the mind and consciousness of the reader in the direction of the communist tasks of the proletariat." In this somewhat tamed condition he certainly roared louder than any wild one ever did, but nobody has pretended that his voice was comparable to that of the original Vladimir Maiakovsky.

The communist explanation of the slight crack—or even, you might say, bleat—which began to be detected in some of the high notes on the Left Front of the Arts, was of course simple. Maiakovsky, even though on the other side of the barricade from Marinetti, had been after all only a futurist, a rebel against bourgeois society, a Bohemian dissenter, not a revolutionist—he naturally could not find his voice in a proletarian society. And ten to one the communist who told you this had himself not been even a rebel or dissenter, but a quite decent citizen of bourgeois society, and had learned all this glib talk about Maiakovsky since he joined the party last year. A poet can find his voice almost anywhere, and a great deal quicker than a party politician. But the voice he finds must be his very own. I do not believe there has ever been a theory of artistic culture which pretended that great art could be produced without the integrated co-operation of the artist's whole personality. That at least, so far as my experience goes, is one unquestionable truth to be found in the field of æsthetics. There is not the slightest reason in the world why in a proletarian society a poet should not be born and live and sing greatly on the theme of shooting the classic generals, and be greatly enjoyed by proletarians, as by all alert citizens, for the brilliancy and relative wisdom of the thought. Maiakovsky might have been that poet if the dupes of practicality had left him alone, and the proletarian culture would have been richer in variety for his songs. But these dupes told him: "There is just one tune, and that is what you've got to sing if you want bread-and-butter, to say nothing of public recognition, so get on the job and sing the right tune."

It is impossible to exaggerate the extent and depth of the earth-quaking storm which swept all thinking Russia when, with Lenin's death, Stalin suddenly barged forward, grabbed the power and the printing presses, and began his job of reducing Trotsky, by force of mere daily and hourly uncontradicted asseveration of lies, from the position of national military hero and intellectual and literary leader of the Bolsheviks to that of an untrustworthy intruder, an alien, a non-Bolshevik, a Menshevik, a bourgeois, a counter-revolutionist, a state prisoner, a traitor, an exile, a man deprived of citizenship and banished for life. In this nation-wide storm of feeling, which swept down all landmarks and left a bleak world intellectually, few men stood up for long. And literary men, generally speaking, as Julien Benda has ably lamented, are not by nature heroes in a brainstorm. The one big character here was Sosnovsky, chief liaison officer under Lenin between the party and the literary world, and he sits today in solitary confinement in a Siberian prison.

Maiakovsky bent his neck to this storm and behaved discreetly. But nevertheless there he was, an independent figure plainly visible on the horizon. Moreover he had his own organization, and kept on putting forth loud thoughts in the name of the "Left Front of the Arts." It is needless to say that every possible pressure was brought to bear on this half-way tamed animal to drive him into the fold along with the curly lambs—now long ago cured of their love-themes, of course, and bleating *agitki* to order as innocent of love or any other impulse of nature, except those for which even artists in uniform must occasionally, I suppose, be excused, as tin-soldiers in a nursery school. Maiakovsky stood wavering under this pressure for a long time. He swung and shifted with a crude dexterity in relation to his own organization, to his own opinions, still seeking some way to be a big thing, as he had a need and a right to be, and yet not surrender the last string of his lyre—the last pipe, rather, of his steam-calliope—to this monster of mental vulgarization and machine politics. I see him gradually driven in, storming and yapping and growling, jumping first this way and then that, crawling rearward, twitching, getting his belly lower and lower to the earth, and finally making a great sudden roaring leap of it and arriving, big and ferocious as ever—so it seemed—in the cage and harness that the dupes of practicality and party hacks were holding ready for him.

It was in the winter of 1930 that Maiakovsky made his great decision, joined the now infamous RAPP, and began to contribute his writings to the *Komsomolskaia Pravda,* acknowledging his poems by that token to be straight journalistic party-propaganda, nothing more. *The Literary Gazette* for February 10th, in which the gleeful politicians announce this "colossal victory of proletarian literature on its road to hegemony," contains a four-column feature-story advertising an exhibition of Maiakovsky's works, with reproduced photographs of early editions, etc., under a giant headline, "The Road of a Great Revolutionary Poet"—a nation-wide official endorsement and *réclame* such as most poets vainly hope may follow when they're dead. The article concludes:

> "Before Maiakovsky lies a broad road. . . .
> Maiakovsky has manifested revolutionary consist-
> ency. He remains a poet fighter, and now he can
> and must merge his creative energy in the creative
> will of the worker mass which is transforming the
> world."

A more honest conclusion to this sudden burst of
official flattery would have been: Maiakovsky, you have
come across at last, and here in our very next issue is your
reward.

Maiakovsky's new road was as short as it was broad. He
announced his surrender to the politicians in a poem
bearing the now pathetic title: *With All My Voice.*

> *"Listen,*
> *comrade posterity:*
> *I the agitator*
> *of the loud-voiced chief,*
> *deafening the floods of poetry,*
> *will step across*
> *the little lyric booklets*
> *as a live man*
> *talking to the living."*

So begins his thunderous manifesto of defeat—destined
to fold up its thunder and hang among the saddest relics
in the temple of the martyred poets. And it concludes,
still thundering:

"Showing up in the Tz.K.K.*
of the coming luminous years,
over the heads
of the gang
of poet grabbers and go-getters,
I will lift up
as a Bolshevik party card
a hundred volumes of my party books."

Maiakovsky read this momentous poem of his, this ultimate surrender of the independent rights of art, at a meeting of the Moscow section of RAPP in early February, 1930. Instead of fulfilling his promise of a hundred volumes of those "party" books, he shot himself through the heart two months later without issuing another line —except this, which he left on the table.

As they say
"the incident is closed."
Love boat
smashed against mores.
I'm quits with life.
No need itemizing
mutual griefs
woes
offenses.
Good luck and goodbye.

Nothing could better prove the significance of this act than the obscene haste with which the politicians, so

* Tzay-Kah-Kah—Central Control Committee.

briefly triumphant, rushed in with a denial that it had any significance. Under a memorial portrait of the dead poet in the party paper the next morning—as a title to the picture, so that none should miss it—were these guilty words:

"The preliminary data of the investigation show that the suicide was due to causes of a purely personal character, having nothing to do with the social or literary activity of the poet."

"This is the same as saying," remarks Trotsky, "that the voluntary death of Maiakovsky was in no way related to his life, or that his life had nothing in common with his revolutionary-poetic creative work—in a word, to turn his death into an event out of the police records. Not true, not necessary, and not clever."

The truth is that the preliminary investigation revealed nothing at all, and the politicians had no data whatever when they wrote that revealing caption under Maiakovsky's picture. This was made clear in the very next column where a member of their staff, the official party poet Demian Byedny, says frankly that he has not the slightest idea why Maiakovsky shot himself. Except as a "temporary lapse of consciousness," he confesses, "an acute psychosis, I am at a loss to explain it."

"Inunderstandable, irremediable, inadmissible," said the orators beside the grave. "Here was some inner conflict, some dissonance."

Two years later, in a memorial article in the Literary Gazette, the truth begins to peep through:

"The death of Maiakovsky showed how great was still his inner contradiction, how strong in him were still the petty bourgeois individualistic forces which he had wished to strangle by attacking the throat of his own song."

Is it not truly wonderful how those words *petty bourgeois* explain everything, and make everything fair and neat and comfortable and nicely all right—everything except the poor dead proletarian poet Kuznetsov! He can not be explained at all. Nothing at all can be done with him. He is no use to anybody—to the dialectician as a category, to the politician as a dreadful example. He is just a dead worker who sang. And so in the memorial literature of the proletariat—such is the irony of fate, or of bureaucracy in politics and bigotry in religion—he must be forgotten.

It is not necessary to pretend to understand too well the immediate cause of Maiakovsky's suicide. Pretending to understand the poetry of the Cult of Unintelligibility is a cheap substitute for criticism, even when no vital questions are at stake. Let us leave that where Maiakovsky did, with his accustomed enigmatic brilliance: "Love boat smashed against *mores*." People rarely kill themselves for one sole reason.

The *mores* against which Maiakovsky went to smash were those of the intra-party dictatorship under Stalin. We know from his own previous poem that the fundamental conflict in him, the dissonance, through all those years had been between the great poet true to his own vision that he desired to be, and the "grabber and go-getter" who made his way by conforming to these hostile *mores*. We know this, if we know enough to talk about the matter at all. For nothing could obtrude more plainly than the self-confession in those lines: "Over the heads of the poet grabbers and go-getters" I will lift up my party card. It was patent at that time to every seeing man—Stalin's politburo confessed it only two years later—that the poet grabbers and go-getters were grabbing at nothing so avidly as at what was summed up in that party card, and that those who were still trying to live for their true vision even of the revolution, were unpaid, unpublished, unacknowledged. The question is not whether Maiakovsky betrayed his motives in those lines, but whether he betrayed them consciously or not. How naïve after all *was* Maiakovsky to pen such bitter irony against himself?

That also I will not pretend to know. I know only that Yessenin, who tried to join the revolution and not surrender his lyre to its political organization, ended in suicide, and that Maiakovsky, who tried to surrender, arrived at the same death. And I know that the similar deaths of these two great poets, whatever the immediate causes, will stand in history as a symbol of the devastation wrought in their decade by the twin monsters, Marxian bigotry and Stalinist bureaucracy, as surely as the similar deaths of Pushkin and Lyermontov have stood symbolic of the foul breath of tzarism and its tool of orthodox religion in their time.

CHAPTER VII

ART TRIES TO BE A HERMIT

ONE OF THE MOST FORTHRIGHT AND EXTREME ASSERTIONS of the independent rights of art was that of the "Serapion Fraternity," a literary group formed almost immediately after the October revolution. This group—whose name derives from a cycle of tales by the German romantic novelist, E. T. A. Hoffmann—was born in the celebrated "literary studio" of the House of the Arts, an institution in Leningrad presided over by Maxim Gorky. The House of the Arts was, in those early days, very influential among intellectual circles, having its own magazine, and making a bold struggle against literary servilism. The informal group who called themselves the Serapion Fraternity were but a part of this general tendency, itself not a new thing in the Russian movement. The eminence of the group was due to the high creative talents possessed by many of its members.

Most of the Serapions, moreover, had fought in the ranks of the Red Army. They were active revolutionists. A majority were fervently interested in the progress of the revolution, and it is universally agreed, even by the champions of the "party line in poetry," that much of the literature most valued by the communist party has been produced by them. This is admitted by the party critics with surprise, or is even advanced against the Serapions as though it proved that they were wrong in their declaration of creative independence. It proves, of course, that they were right. I do not mean that they were right in all the details of their absolute and hermit-like and somewhat Quakerish announcements. They were right in refusing to put on an art-uniform after taking off the uniforms of soldiers. They were right in asserting the principle of variety as fundamental in the arts. It is because creative art, like life itself at leisure, seeks variety, that artists in uniform are self-destroying and ridiculous. They were right in refusing to be judged by politicians and as propagandists. They were right—and they were prophetic—in featuring *sincerity* as the precious thing most imminently in the risk of being lost. And they were right in putting these views forth in the extreme language of intellectual courage and conviction—a language since all but disused in Soviet Russia.

"Critics," they said, "demand of the Serapions a party ideology. The proletarian writers who have it are bad writers. Each of the Serapions has his own individual ideology. Works of art organically are good with no matter what ideology. Art lives its own life and has no ultimate goal. Art is meaningless to politicians. Men of politics want only an art which works upon society—that is, journalism. We, the Serapions, will not be journalists. We demand one thing: that the voice should not ring false."

"We assembled in the days of the revolution, in the days of mighty political tension," wrote one of their number in 1922. " 'Whoever is not with us is against us,' people were telling us from right and left. 'With whom then are you Serapion Brothers? With the communists or against the communists, for the revolution or against the revolution?'

" 'With whom then are you, Serapion Brothers?'

" 'We are with the Hermit Serapion.'

" 'That is, you are with nobody? That is, the swamp? That is, intellectual æsthetes? Without ideology, without conviction? 'Our hut is on the edge of the town and we know nothing'?

" 'No.'

" 'Each one of us has his ideology, his political conviction, each paints his hut in his own color. Thus it is in life. And thus in tales, in stories, dramas. We all together, however—as a brotherhood—demand one thing . . . that we should believe in the reality of the production, whatever color it may wear. . . .'

" 'And one thing more unites us, not to be demonstrated or explained—our fraternal love.' "

The relative weight of this group, as judged from the standpoint of talent, may be estimated from the following statement made by Trotsky in 1923:

"If we should eliminate Pilnyak, with his *The Bare Year*, the Serapion Fraternity with Vsevolod Ivanov, Tikhonov, and Polonskaia, if we should eliminate Maiakovsky and Yessenin, is there anything that will remain for us but a few unpaid promissory notes of a future proletarian literature?"

Trotsky admonished the Serapions of the danger of

drifting away from the revolution through their unwill-
ingness to ally their art with its policies. "Critical periods," he said, "do not allow an artist the luxury of an
automatic and irresponsible elaboration of social points
of view. And whoever boasts of this . . . is masking a reactionary tendency or has fallen into social stupidities or
is making a fool of himself." The Serapions did not lower
their banners to this political criticism, influential
though it then was, nor did they faint before Trotsky's
demonstration that they had "approached the revolution
from the wrong side, that of the peasant." To anyone who
understands the relation between art and life, it is not
sensible to talk about having approached the revolution
from the "wrong side." Does not mankind, in those moments of realization, those moments which he can devote
to the enlargement of his experience through art, desire
among other things the experience of the revolution as
approached from the side of the peasant? Has he not a
right to this phase of experience poignantly rendered?
Can an artist, moreover, who actually did approach the
revolution from the side of the peasant, possibly produce
great art while repudiating his own experience out of
loyalty to the revolution as "a conception, an organization, a plan, a work"? In some rare instance of intellectual and homiletic poetry he might, or in some work devoted to portraying, not the revolution, but that very
effort of mental development. In general he could not.
"The Marxian methods are not the same as the artistic."
The conceptions, organizations, plans, and works of an
engineering corps, moreover, are not the same thing as
the realizations of an artist—and this is as true in the

field of politics as of mechanics. The Serapions knew this, and they were not dismayed by political criticisms, no matter how authoritative.

It was not until Trotsky himself, with his flexible understanding of Marxism, was swept aside and those admonitory criticisms caught up and brandished as a club by an organization determined to "control" proletarian literature, and "determine its manifestation" through sheer physical possession of the presses and publishing houses, that these Serapions—with one notable exception—lowered their clear banner of art's independence. A quotation from the two successive leaders of the *At-Your-Post* group who under Stalin "seized the power in literature" will show what force subdued them.

Rodov: "We think that the party, at whatever cost, ought to *dominate the literary movement of the working class,* and all remaining problems, problems of literary artistic criticism or any other party problems . . . should be raised only after the final solution of this fundamental problem."

Auerbach: "We can and ought to cooperate, set the scenes, surround the worker writers with the necessary atmosphere, influence, and to a certain degree—*we have the press, the publishing houses, etc.—determine the manifestation of the new literature."* *

That phrase, "We have the press, the publishing houses, etc."—spoken in 1924 at the beginning of a baleful career—denotes, of course, the essence of the force that subdued the Serapions, and subdued all other independent artistic impulses, subdued, destroyed or ban-

* The italics in both cases are mine.

ished them. Yet that frank phrase gives no hint of the epidemic fury of the public assault subsequently stirred up by these joy-hating functionaries, who sought out and stamped to death as though it were a pestilence or dreadful conflagration, every residual flicker of the idea that art has some function to perform besides the propagation of a party faith and a machine loyalty. Their methods recall those of the Black Hundreds. Even those who imagine that only by these methods could the workers' republic have been held together after Lenin's death, would do well, if they are sincerely interested in the future of mankind, to recognize this fact. For the difference between class struggle guided by professional revolutionists with moral and intellectual authority, and public hysteria engineered by bureaucrats appealing to the greed, fear, hatred, and bigotry of men, will be of vital import in the times to come.

The distribution of heroic moral fibre is at least not greater among artists, than among the common run of men. We need not be surprised, therefore, that Vsevolod Ivanov, a boisterous and magnetic writer of colorful stories, gradually forgot under Stalin these principles proclaimed so loudly under Lenin and Trotsky. "I think that the 'classic' days are gone for good," he now says, "and that thematics of the day ought to predominate in our work." Tikhonov, too, has no wish left, but that art may become a "reflection" of "our cultural reconstruction and industrialism." Slonimsky, another prominent Serapion, now looks to literature for "the consolidation of the forces of the proletariat."

It is no task of mine to judge the "sincerity" of these

artists of the Serapion faith. Whether they were swept honestly along in the social brainstorm, or whether they put up these statements of opinion as a small personal shelter against the storm, only their own hearts can tell. The nature of the storm, however, and the fate of any man heroic enough to stand publicly against it, can be seen in the experience of an early teacher and inspirer of the group, Eugene Zamyatin.

CHAPTER VIII

THE FRAMING OF EUGENE ZAMYATIN

ZAMYATIN IS UNIQUE AMONG RUSSIAN WRITERS—PRO-phetic to my mind of something literature has still to attain. For besides being a gifted and imaginative artist, he is a trained man of science. He was a working Bolshevik when most of those who subsequently denounced him in the name of the "Bolshevik creative line" were still in school. Active in the revolution of 1905, he was arrested and served his time in solitary confinement. Nor did his zeal die in the period of lapse and reaction. His training as a naval engineer in the Polytechnic Institute was continually interrupted by the authorities, and it was during a period of exile that he first began to write. His writing was an avocation, however, and his profession the construction of ice-cutting vessels, until he returned to Russia from England in the fall of 1917. After the October revolution he taught science in the Polytechnic Institute, but gave his main energy and ingenuity to writing, and to editing literary journals, and to gathering talented people together with a view to building a great literature in the new Russia.

Being a man of intellect, however, and moreover a man of scientific intellect, Zamyatin's conception of literature is a large one, and not at all consonant with the view that all ultimate wisdom resides in the secretariat of a political party.

"A living literature," says Zamyatin, "lives not in the hours of yesterday nor of today, but of tomorrow. It is a sailor sent aloft on the mast where he can see shipwrecks, icebergs and maelstroms still invisible from the deck. . . . What we need now in literature is colossal look-out views, airplane philosophic views; we need the most ultimate, the most terrible, the most unterrified *whys?* and *what furthers?* . . . Were there in nature anything immoveable, were there truths, all this of course would be incorrect. But fortunately all truths are erroneous: the dialectic process consists in this, that today's truths become tomorrow's errors. There is no final number.

"This (single) truth is only for the strong. . . . The weak-nerved lack the power to include themselves in the dialectic syllogism. It is difficult, indeed. But that is just what Einstein did. He managed to remember that he, Einstein, watching motions with a watch in his hand, is also in motion. He managed to look upon earthly motions from without. It is so that a great literature, one which knows no final number, will look upon earthly motions."

With these ideals, and a training in constructive science, it is not surprising that Zamyatin wants to say something in his books about the larger destinies of man.

He wants to say something about what is to come *after* the technique of capitalist machine-industry has been taken over by a successful proletarian revolution and developed to the full. His romance, *We,* published in English in 1924, is an inverse utopia of the type subsequently exemplified in Aldous Huxley's *Brave New World.* Indeed its theme is identical with Huxley's, the unhappy situation of poetic people in that complete regimentation of life toward which science seems to lead the way. It is, however, a more recklessly imaginative book than Huxley's and its imaginations are realized with a greater depth of feeling. Zamyatin in 1924 considered *We* "at once the most jocular and the most earnest thing" he had written, and it is evidently the heart-spoken message of a man of poetry who has delved deeply in science.

Zamyatin could not find a publisher for his *magnum opus* in Soviet Russia—not because it was counter-revolutionary, there is not a counter-revolutionary line in it —but because it was untimely. The Bolsheviks did not want to dwell on the problem of the "creative personality" in a civilization which "depends upon the energetic movement of great masses of people"—to quote the English translator—at a time when all their attention was engaged in the task of moving great masses of people. In that they were doubtless right. But Zamyatin read his book to the Authors' League in Moscow, and gave notice in the Soviet press of its English publication. It was commented upon by Soviet critics and for six years no protest against its publication was ever uttered. The best proof that Zamyatin has written nothing anti-Soviet or counter-revolutionary, lies in the fact that in 1929 a Moscow publishing house began the publication of his Complete Works. His heresy consists essentially in loving dispassionate reflection, and believing in the value of heresy as such. His sin is all summed up—together with the bigotry of those who condemned him—in the following passage from the Greater Soviet Encyclopedia:

> "Zamyatin does not accept the social revolution; it is for him only a link in a chain of universal cosmic revolutions. (sic!) 'The social revolution (he says) is only one of an infinite number; the law of revolution is not a social, but an infinitely greater cosmic universal law. We must look upon earthly movements from without. Heretics are the sole (bitter) medicine against the entropy of human thought.' These phrases conceal the writer's unbelief and non-acceptance of the social revolution."

When encyclopedias talk like that, you can imagine how the party politicians talk! Zamyatin's crime was that he kept his intellectual independence and moral integrity. He refused as an artist to take orders from a political bureaucracy. He was moreover, with Boris Pilnyak, the most active leader of that All Russian Union of Writers, or genuine Authors' League, which alone resisted RAPP and blocked the road to its control of Russian arts and letters. Therefore the word went out for his destruction.

In the Autumn of 1929, returning from a summer's travel, Zamyatin found that he had been made, together with Pilnyak, the victim of a frame-up. A charge of collaboration with émigré Social Revolutionaries—which means state treason—had been published in the official weekly *Literary Gazette,* and "all soviet sociality" summoned to condemn him for an "act" which he had never committed, nor could possibly have dreamed of committing. No American can (as yet), even with the memory of the Liberty Loan hysterias, imagine the devastating ferocity of these campaigns in the party-controlled press in Stalin's Russia to "destroy" a man or bring him to his knees before the throne of power. The forces unleashed are nation-wide and automatic as machine guns, and there is no shelter for the victim. No printed word can appear in his defense. Not even a demand that the matter be investigated can be publicly put forward by his friends. Zamyatin was not only denounced in the official press from one end of the Soviet Union to the other as a counter-revolutionist and a traitor, but was condemned in a panic, without a hearing and without even an investigation, by his comrades of the Authors' League.

The facts underlying the frame-up are extremely simple. Chapters of Zamyatin's book, *We,* were pirated by a Social Revolutionary journal in Czechoslovakia, and printed—at first without his knowledge, and as soon as he knew it, *against his protest.* Upon this ground, and this only, he was accused of "collaborating with White Guard circles beyond the border." He knew well, as all Russian writers did, that a refutation of the charge would avail him nothing. He had but one choice: either to repudiate his own creation—and for a man of cloudier character that would have been easy after nine years—or cease his literary and social existence in the Soviet Union. Zamyatin chose the path of the artist's integrity. He wrote a letter to the *Literary Gazette,* stating the facts in the case with simple dignity—the sole words in his defense that ever found their way into print—resigned from the Authors' League, and in a short time, as was inevitable, left Russia to live in exile in Paris. His letter, printed in the *Literary Gazette* of October 7, 1929, reads as follows:

"When I returned to Moscow after a summer journey the whole affair of my book, *We,* was finished. It was already established that the appearance of fragments from *We* in the publication *Volia Rossii* of Prague was my act, and in regard to this 'act' all the necessary resolutions had been adopted.

"But facts are stubborn. They are more stubborn than resolutions. Every one of them may be confirmed by documents or people, and I wish to make them known to my readers. . . .

"1. The novel, *We,* was written in 1920. In 1921 the manuscript was sent (in the simplest manner, in a registered package through the Petrograd Post Office) to Berlin to the publishers Grzhebin. This publishing house had then a department in Berlin, Moscow, and Petrograd, and I was bound by contracts with this publisher.

"2. At the end of 1923 a copy of this manuscript was made by the publisher for translation into the English language (this translation appeared before 1925), and afterward into Czecho-Slovak. I gave notice of these translations in the Russian press several times. . . . Comments about it were also printed in the Soviet papers. I have never heard one protest upon the subject of these translations.

"3. In 1924 it became known that, owing to the censorship, the novel *We* could not be printed in Soviet Russia. In view of this I declined all proposals to publish *We* abroad in the Russian language. Such propositions I received both from Grzhebin and also later from the publisher, Petropolis. . . .

"4. In the spring of 1927 fragments from *We* appeared in the Prague magazine *Volia Rossii*. I. G. Ehrenburg was comradely enough to advise me of this in a letter from Paris. It was thus that I first learned of my 'act.'

"5. At that time, the summer of 1927, Ehrenburg at my request sent to the editors of *Volia Rossii* a letter demanding in my name that they stop printing fragments from *We*. . . . *Volia Rossii* refused to accede to my demands.

"6. From Ehrenburg I learned one more thing: the fragments printed in *Volia Rossii* were supplied with a preface informing the reader that the novel was being printed in a translation from Czech into Russian. . . . It is obvious to the most modest logic that such an operation upon an artistic creation could not be performed with the knowledge and consent of the author.

"That is the whole of my 'act.' Is this similar to what has been written about it in the newspapers (for example, in the Leningrad *Pravda* where the direct statement appears: 'Eugene Zamyatin gave *carte blanche* to *Volia Rossii* to publish his story *We*')?

"The literary campaign against me was launched by an article of Volin in No. 19 of the *Literary Gazette*. Volin forgot to say in his article that he remembered about my novel, *We,* nine years late (for the novel, as I said, was written in 1920).

"In his article Volin forgot to say that he remembered about the printing of fragments of my novel, *We,* in *Volia Rossii* two and one-half years late (for these fragments, as I said, were printed in the spring of 1927).

"And finally Volin forgot to speak of the editor's preface in *Volia Rossii,* from which it is clear that the fragments from the novel were printed without my knowledge and consent.

"That is the 'act' of Volin. Whether these silences were conscious or accidental I do not know, but their consequence was an untruthful presentation of the facts.

"The matter was taken up in the executive bureau of the Union of Soviet Writers, and the resolution of the executive bureau was published in No. 21 of the *Literary Gazette*. In section 2, the executive bureau 'decisively condemns the act of the above named writers,' Pilnyak and Zamyatin. In section 4 of the same resolution, the executive bureau advises the Leningrad department of the Union to 'investigate directly the circumstances of the publication abroad of Zamyatin's novel, *We.*'

Thus we have first a condemnation, and afterward an investigation. No court in the world, I daresay, ever heard of such a procedure. That is the 'act' of the Union of Writers.

"Further the question of the printing of my novel in *Volia Rossii* was taken up in a general meeting of the Moscow branch of the All-Russian Union of Writers, and afterward in a general meeting of the Leningrad branch.

"The Moscow meeting, without waiting for my explanations or even expressing a desire to hear them, adopted a resolution condemning that same 'act.' The members of the Moscow branch also found it timely to express their protest in regard to the contents of a novel written nine years before and unknown to the majority of the members. In our times nine years is essentially nine ages. I am not going to defend here a novel nine ages old. I merely think that if the Moscow members of the Union had protested against the novel, *We,* six years ago, when the novel was read at one of the literary evenings of the Union, that would have been more timely.

"The general assembly of the Leningrad branch of the Union was called on September 22nd, and I know of its results only through newspaper notices. . . . From these notices it is evident that in Leningrad my explanations had been read, and that here the opinion of those present was divided. A number of the writers, after my explanation, considered the whole incident closed. But the majority found it more prudent to condemn my 'act.' Such was the 'act' of the All-Russian Union of Writers, and from this act I draw my conclusion:

"To belong to a literary organization which, even indirectly, takes part in the persecution of a co-member, is impossible for me, and I hereby announce my withdrawal from the All-Russian Union of Writers."

EUGENE ZAMYATIN
Moscow, Sept. 24, 1929.

To appreciate the clear-headed and courageous dignity of this letter, you must again remember that the charge against Zamyatin was equivalent to state treason, that this charge had been authoritatively published throughout the length and breadth of the land, and that Zamyatin well knew no presentation of the facts would get it revoked. He knew that nothing in the world would get it revoked but a recantation and repudiation by him of his own writings. He must "acknowledge his mistake" —so runs the formula of servility, most hideous burlesque of Lenin's honesty of mind—or be destroyed. It would seem to belong neither to "proletarian" nor "bourgeois" morality, but to the most elementary decencies of human intercourse, having falsely charged a man not only with a sneaking disloyalty but with a crime punishable by death, to revoke the charge when confronted with unanswerable facts to the contrary. It does not belong to the morality of Stalin. His editorial tool, Volin, had nothing to say in reply to the above letter, but that Zamyatin was "putting the main question off with chronology and refusing to stick to the point," and that the fact was well established that he "had not renounced his book."

"If Eugene Zamyatin continues haughtily to persist in his mistake," reads the official decree, "then the last threads uniting him with Soviet sociality will be severed."

In the *Literary Gazette* for October 11th, the usual series of "monolithic" condemnations from a whole series of writers' organizations throughout the Soviet Union— people who could never have read Zamyatin's book in English or Czechoslovak and knew absolutely nothing of its publication—was introduced editorially with the following remarks: "Eugene Zamyatin, with his letter presenting the affair as though anybody in the world had perpetrated his 'acts,' but not he, has opposed himself to the whole of Soviet sociality. Eugene Zamyatin, and through his example every writer, ought to understand this simple thought, that a country building socialism can get along perfectly well without a writer whose popularity among the toilers is far from envious, but not one writer living in this country and wishing to make his creations valuable can fail to take part in the active work of socialist construction. Eugene Zamyatin ought to draw the conclusion and communicate it to our writers and to 'his readers' as publicly as he has communicated the dates and facts of the history of his novel, *We*. The further attitude to him of Soviet writers and of all Soviet sociality will depend upon his choice."

That was the end of Zamyatin—and of the dangerous opinion that the "social revolution is only one link in a chain of universal cosmic revolutions."

A fitting benediction will be found in the Chapter on Soviet Art in Ella Winter's recent book, *Red Virtue*:

"The idea that artists are forced to do what the State wants is as untrue as the legend that women are nationalized."

Miss Winter quotes from Lenin's remarks to Clara Zetkin—"Every artist, everybody who wishes to, can claim the right to create freely according to his ideal, whether it turn out good or not"—and is fond enough to tell us this describes conditions under Stalin.

CHAPTER IX

ROMANOV'S RECANTATION

SOME READERS WILL NO DOUBT IMAGINE THAT I AM PRESENT-ing a one-sided view of the matter in discussion, that the writers I select for comment are not typical. They will tell me about the colorful stories and plays of Vsevolod Ivanov, about the vivid work done by Lidin, Fadeev, Panferov, the sea-yarns of Novikov-Priboy, about Leonov, Olyesha, Alexei Tolstoy, about the delicate poems of Boris Pasternak. Perhaps they will venture to mention Panteleimon Romanov, and quote me this remark from the *New Statesman* of London: "It is one of the mysteries of Soviet government that Romanov's books are allowed to be published. . . . The enforced intimacies, the hideous lack of privacy, the gross stupidity of its rulers, the dreadful struggle with poverty, are all displayed here passionately and with an imaginative power that we expect from Romanov."

I am aware that a number of excellent books have been written in Russia during this past decade. Some have been written by men whose natural genius is for a narrow, practical loyalty. There is, after all, a sincere literature of bigotry. Others have been written by men and women who, like Art Young in this country, remain instinctively remote from the concrete battle of opinion.

A conflict between some American Lenin and Martov might settle the future of the revolution for a hundred years, but Art Young would hardly be involved in it. His business is with the generalities of the socialist idea. There are men like that in Russia—among them Vsevolod Ivanov. Maxim Gorky, chastened by his innumerable political mistakes in the past, now contents himself with this somewhat detached position. Made almost inviolable by his international prestige and the memory of his early friendship with Lenin, he is grudgingly permitted to play the patriarch—although not without an occasional reminder that the eye of the Inquisition is on him.

"Gorky did not escape scrutiny at the hands of these zealots," says Alexander Kaun in his authorized biography, after describing the activities of RAPP. "In a number of articles and in literary text-books he was subjected to an inquisition and found wanting as a proletarian writer. Among the evidence against him was advanced the fact that as a child he was brought up in a petty-bourgeois family, and that most of the years before he became a writer he spent as a tramp and a jack-of-all-trades, rather than as a legitimate factory worker. As to his writings, it was pointed out that he failed in drawing proletarian characters, rendering them sweetish and unreal. He was reproached for devoting his post-revolutionary fiction to problems and scenes of the past, rather than portraying the glorious present. Of course, he was taken to account for his heresies, defections, and disloyalties. He was declared a fellow-traveler, and one who lived abroad, in the bourgeois West, to boot. . . ."

Gorky came off so lightly for particular reasons—in part, no doubt, exactly because his writings are in the past or treat of it. There are other phases of literature, however, precisely contemporary, yet so close to mere entertainment or diversion as to flourish happily, like the circus or the athletic games, no matter who may "seize the power in poetry." All these manifestations are irrelevant to my theme. My theme is that, what with bigotry of Marxist metaphysics and brutality of Stalinist bureaucratism, literature as a vitally incisive, thinking human function with the push of growth in it, has been silenced, watered down, or banished, or destroyed. In proof I have promised to cite the example of the two or three most eminent talents in each broad field of literary art, and this seems to me a fair procedure. I could, however, fill up another book with slightly less eminent examples.

I could tell, for instance, the surprising story of how even Demian Byedny, the propaganda singer *in excelsis*, the poetic staff-officer of the revolution, was of a sudden boxed on the ears by the all-powerful Auerbach and demoted. In the beginning the Inquisitors had put up Demian Byedny as a model. They had preached, in fact, that they were going to "demianize" all art and literature. But Demian, although within reasonable limits a humble servant of the bureaucracy, turned out after all to have some guts. He insisted at least on having personal control of semicolons. As Trotsky put it, when this amazing thing occurred: "Demian is willing to play the lackey—but so-to-speak on a wholesale, not a retail, plan. To catch up every paper of instruction, every little zigzag, to sweep up the litter of yesterday's work, to tremble sweetly at the eloquence of Koganovich—no, he is not quite capable of that. For that kind of job there are plenty of nameless people old and new. And so the Auerbachs received a sudden and complete illumination: 'Not only is it unnecessary to demianize literature, but Demian himself must be undemianized to the last shred.' "

Or I could tell another interesting story—that of the mirthful satirist, Valentine Kataev, who dared to believe that life is beautiful and "justifies itself" from the very fact of its being life, and who "in consequence gave an important place in his writings to love." I could tell how this "philistinism" was scared out of him by the Inquisitors, and from being a satirist with flashes of genius, he was converted into a faithful Sunday School moralist of the five-year plan—a slight excess of unction, an overcorrection of that inborn gift of irony, the one thing left to remember it by.

"What is the social meaning of this philosophy of 'immediate life' which is 'wonderful' and 'self-justified'?" asks the Lesser Encyclopedia. (And I quote these encyclopedias, not because I am unaware of the more virulent polemics combined with broad hints of a practical nature with which the work was done in the magazines, but because encyclopedias are supposed to represent whatever cool and honest judgment the times afford.) What is the social meaning of this philosophy of the gay young man Kataev? "It is the philosophy of philistinism, the philosophy of people who do not want to make life over, who are tired of struggling with its evil and capable only of enjoying it." And so Kataev, we learn, is now "trying to overcome the philistinism of his earlier creations and draw near to the socialist constructivity." From which we may infer that he is helping to build socialism on the hypothesis that life is *not* wonderful and does *not* justify itself, though what could bring any sane man to bother with the building of socialism on that hypothesis, we may fail to understand.

It is impossible for me to go intimately into each of these stories of the inward decomposition of an artist, its fits and starts, its crude excesses and recessions. I am not writing a history of Russian literature. I will not, however, pass over the mention of Panteleimon Romanov.

The passage which I quoted above from the *New Statesman* came of course to the attention of the Inquisitors. They made a photostatic copy of it, reproduced it in the *Literary Gazette*, supplying a Russian translation by way of title, and adding the brief remark that, while P. Romanov "is not responsible for what appears about him in an English review, he is responsible for his book. . . ."

No further word was necessary. The meaning of these few words was clear and understood. If P. Romanov does not drop instantly to his knees and disavow his book—"acknowledge his mistake," that is, in writing it—the end of P. Romanov as a Russian writer and a Russian citizen, a member of "Soviet sociality," is in sight. His previous books will disappear from the bookstores; his future books will be denied publication; he will be attacked in the press as a counter-revolutionist and traitor to the "land of the Soviets"; his social life and fame will be destroyed.

It is as well that we are spared the inner history of P. Romanov in this crisis. There arrived at the office of the editor, after a brief space of time, a document of self-repudiation and repudiation of the essence of poetic art, which, if it were not interpretable as a mockery of the Inquisitors, would sicken the hearts of those who have admired him. His novel, he averred, had been written in order to call attention to certain evils in the state apparatus; the evils had since been attacked by the government and were now—after two years!—completely "cleaned away." Moreover he had made a mistake in calling attention to these evils with concentrated force and vigor of passion—as an artist, that is, should and must—and he would never do it again.

But let us have it in his own words. The novel in question was *Comrade Kissliakov* called *Three Pairs of Silk Stockings* in translation.

"The aim of my novel, written two years ago," he says, "was to show the manifestation of Kissliakov-ism, that is, class-ideological alien elements, hiding under various masks. The purgation which began subsequently and which fundamentally cleaned away from our state apparatus and social life the Kissliakovs, seemed to demonstrate to me that my diagnosis was right. But seeing what interpretations have been put upon my novel both abroad and in Soviet criticism, I have reached the conclusion that a politically mistaken book has actually been written by me. . . .

"My mistake, as I now see, lay in the method at

the bottom of the novel. This method consisted in taking only the phenomenon which interested me and centering upon it the whole force of my attention. I set aside all opposing and weakening impressions or elements in order to pursue this phenomenon to its last depth and compel the reader to contemplate this phenomenon with all his force. I thus violated the normal proportion of life and gave an objectively untrue picture of reality. . . ."

If I were the Inquisitor to receive such a letter from an exquisite artist, I should consider myself not apologized to, but mocked. Comrade Volin, however, was complacent. He was not interested—nor was his master—in the inner consciousness of Panteleimon Romanov. He was interested in his future acts. He deemed it unnecessary, he said, to criticize P. Romanov's explanation of how he came to make his "mistake." He considered *"fundamental* in the letter of P. Romanov his acknowledgment that the novel written by him was *politically erroneous."* "P. Romanov," he added, "has the opportunity in his coming creations of demonstrating the sincerity of the letter printed above."

Or in other words: One more misstep, P. Romanov, and you are done for.

CHAPTER X

THE SILENCE OF ISAAC BABYEL

THE TWO PRINCIPAL EVENTS IN RUSSIAN PROSE FICTION of the last six years are the silence of Isaac Babyel and the humiliation of Boris Pilnyak. Babyel is probably the greater artist of the two. The appearance of his *Odessa Stories* and *Horse Army* (1924–26) is the only event since the revolution which can be described as the arrival of a new star in the zenith. It was so described almost universally. Not only Russia, but all those enjoying "cultural relations" with her, were put in a state of expectancy by the rank tales, recklessly drenched with color, told by this young cavalry soldier, "the greatest Russian stylist since Pushkin," as many dared to say. Why was this world-wide expectancy left hanging in the air? Why did Isaac Babyel turn his back on a fame already international, retire into the background and publish no word, save some recollections of childhood, for five years?

It is difficult to determine the cause of a negative phenomenon. But I believe from my reading that it is because he is an artist and not a recruiting sergeant. He refused to submit to the demand of the hacks and hand-out men of the Stalin regime that he write bally-hoo for the Red Army. No less an authority than General Budyenny demonstrated to the satisfaction of all philistines that Babyel's stories were a libellous "distortion" of the life of the Red Army, and that fact is solemnly chalked against him, not only in the political journals with which RAPP destroyed Russian literature, but even in *The Literary Encyclopedia*, where his sin of being an individual is conscientiously set forth. But Babyel is no girl-baby, to wither up under the literary criticism of an ignorant Rough Rider. Budyenny's cultural interpolations were a party joke in the times of Lenin and Trotsky. What stopped Babyel was the fact that behind these criticisms stood the sinister figure of Auerbach—"We have the printing presses and the publishing houses—we should . . . determine the manifestation of proletarian literature"—and behind Auerbach stood RAPP, and behind RAPP the whole power of the bureaucracy, not interested in RAPP's literary works or theories, but encouraging its bigotries as a tool in the elimination of honest Bolshevik criticism.

Babyel refused to surrender his incomparable pen into the hands of these new slave-drivers of creation, these brigadiers of the boy scouts of poetry, these professional vulgarians prostituting the idea of the liberation of all society by the proletariat to the task of enslaving all utterance and all creative life to an iron-ribbed bureaucratic political machine. He retired to the Ukraine—retired to France—retired to a peasant village. He found some way to keep alive in silence.

He learned that even silence is treasonable when artists are in uniform. "What is the matter with Babyel now? He is not writing anything. We must put the clamps on him," whispered the literary vigilantes. And they did what they could to make him uncomfortable. They eliminated his name from the press, for one thing, almost as completely as though he had died or openly opposed them.

But Babyel is, for various reasons, a privileged character in Soviet Russia. He is protected, in the first place, by Gorky, who regards him as the greatest living Russian prose writer—destined, in some sense, to succeed to his own place of eminence. Babyel has also preserved his connections with the Red Army, and with the GPU, where he worked during the Civil War. I am told that Stalin himself appreciates Babyel and allows him a kind of privilege not unlike that possessed by Gorky. With all these advantages, and with a nature apparently sociable and subtle enough to make the most of them, Babyel has managed throughout the whole period of its florescence to elude the pressure of the Literary Inquisition. He has kept silent, but he has kept his pen in his own hand.

Babyel is a loyal Bolshevik and a great artist. His words will hold a high place of honor in Russian literature—his silence perhaps almost as high a place.

CHAPTER XI

THE HUMILIATION OF BORIS PILNYAK

TO APPRECIATE THE SITUATION IN RUSSIAN LITERATURE, it is necessary to remember not only that the life of the author who will not sell his pen to the bureaucracy is a social misery and a literary death, but that the life of the author who will sell is, as lives go in Russia, luxurious. It is true, as Maurice Hindus states, that authors and playwrights are among the richest people in Russia, and that "whatever the grievances and disabilities of the artist, *if his work is acceptable,* he lives as abundantly as is possible under existing soviet conditions, and he need never worry about a market for his work or an appreciating audience." * Not only does crucifixion await the stiffnecked, but a substantial taste of the kingdoms of this world and the glory of them is offered to those who surrender. A luridly shining example of this is Boris Pilnyak.

"This novelist," says Ella Winter in her naïve chapter about art in Soviet Russia, "is reputed to be one of the richest men in the union; his income is estimated at 30,000 rubles a year. He goes abroad frequently and has travelled in and written about the Orient, the United States and Europe. His books sell in great quantities. Pilnyak is a fellow traveller, no Communist, but he be-

* *The Great Offensive* (italics mine).

trays at times a yearning to be ideologically more in the swim than he is."

Let us examine the history of this "yearning" of Boris Pilnyak.

In 1924, just before the scope and ferocity of the victory of bureaucratism became clear, a small anthology was published in Moscow, entitled, *Artists About Art and About Themselves.* To this anthology Pilnyak contributed some fearless and straight-spoken pages of his diary—notably the following, dated September 28 of the preceding year:

"A big mail, and since morning I have been reading letters and answering them. Again letters about all kinds of lito-politicians—very tiresome that all the world has only one question: Do you acknowledge, or do you not acknowledge?—although this question is as superfluous as whether I acknowledge my own life; here's what I do not acknowledge; I do not acknowledge that it is necessary to write with a gulp every time you mention the Russian Communist Party, as very many do, especially those quasi-communists who are thus giving to our revolution a tone of disagreeable bragging and self-adulation —I do not acknowledge that a writer ought to live 'with a will not to see,' or speaking simply, to be a liar, for lies are what you get when some kind of statistical proportion is not observed. (For example, we have the European-equipped Kashirskaia power station, but half of Russia still lives without kerosene,—so it is obviously more sensible to write that Russia is sitting here in the dark in the evenings, than to write that we have achieved electrification; or another example: I remember in the year 1920 reading in the magazine *Gudok* 'Victory on the labor front! Seventeen wagons of firewood were loaded by the Guberetsky workers'—it seems to me that if you bear in mind the English load-lifting cranes, it would be truer to say:—"Defeat on the labor front.') I am not a communist and therefore I do not acknowledge that I ought to be a communist and write as a communist—and I acknowledge that the communist power in Russia is determined not by the will of communists, but by the historic destinies of Russia, and in so far as I want to follow (according to my ability and as my conscience and mind dictate to me) these Russian historic destinies I am with the communists, that is, in so far as the communists are with Russia, so far I am with them. (Just now, in these days, that means more than ever before, since I have no use for the philistines): I acknowledge that the destinies of the Russian Communist Party are far less interesting to me than the destinies of Russia. The Russian Communist Party for me is only a link in the destiny of Russia. I know that I ought to be absolutely objective, not to pour water in anybody's mill, not to deceive anybody,—and I acknowledge that maybe I am wrong in everything—but also I very well know that I can not write otherwise than I do write. I am unable to, and I will not, even though I should want to violate myself; there is a literary law which makes it impossible to violate a literary talent—even with your own brain—and an example of this is the situation of all our contemporary literature:—Bunin (an excellent writer!) and Merezhkovsky on the right, Serafimovich on the left, old writers, are writing nothing or writing very badly, because they have substituted politics for art, they write in the name of politics and their art is not art at all, it has lost its ring:—our state power has installed in these recent years incubators for party literature, supplied them with rations—and nothing has come of it, and even harm has come of it, for these people coming in contact with art, have ceased to be politicians without becoming artists—and the young literature has arrived in solitary figures, nobody knows whence, self-produced without midwives, and there have come various kinds of people, muzhikized anarchists and defeated intellectuals and communists—they have all come, without passports to such and such literary rank or such and such party membership, but with the sound money of their manuscripts, in which it is told how our present life sounds to them: and hence one more inference—I acknowledge that the writer ought to occupy himself only with his manuscripts, to see to it that they are good, and as to what kind of honesty and valor pertains to his party-educational-social-service ticket, that is his private business having no relation to literature; and life confirms this rule of mine—we have in Moscow the devil knows how many kinds of literary schools (even party-literary), I cannot count their names, but I can count the good poets and writers. They are fewer than the names of schools, and the majority of them—to what schools do they belong?—I think they belong to the school of their own talents—and it is not a writer's business to think up various passports; let the historians of literature afterward distribute us in our respective regiments for convenience of study."

These statements were not originally made for publication, and their candor can hardly be questioned. They are the last words of Pilnyak about literature, or about politics, or about "lito-politicians," or about himself, or about anything whatever bearing upon the subject of creative art and communism, as to which this can be said. Pilnyak has not only become "one of the richest men in Russia"; he has simultaneously become Russia's leading expert in recantation, abjection, self-repudiation, sighs of repentance and prayers of apology for the sin of having had thoughts, impulses, fancies, emotions, reactions, reflexes, tropisms, or any perceptible knee-jerks or eyewinks that he could call his own. The literary journals are soggy with his unctuous promises and tears of contrition. He begs for Marxian instruction. He asks to have special censors appointed to watch over his novels and dissect out in advance any malignant matter foreign to the policies of the party. He promises in one winter to bring as his offering to the proletariat a book "showing how American capitalism looks to the eye and feeling" and a novel portraying "the past and present course of the history of the capitalist countries and the Soviet Union from the founding of the Soviet Union (and the Versailles Peace) to the days of the five-year plan and the world crisis." He is so glib with apologies, and watery with tears of contrition, that his enemies will tell you he is playing for the day of the counter-revolution. "Didn't you see I was mocking them all the time?" he will say.

Of this explanation I have my doubts. Pilnyak is an easy and yet enigmatical character—enigmatical, perhaps, because that makes things easy in the circumstances surrounding him. The idea of his planning for a single winter a book on American capitalism and a history of capitalism and communism since the Versailles Treaty, is funny. And so are his exaggerated self-abnegations funny, if you do not care vitally about art or character. There is probably, therefore, some irony mixed with his obsequiousness, as there was in Heine's letter "To the Most Noble Federal Diet." But Pilnyak is not gambling on a dubious future. He is trying to *save himself now*—save some small shred or relic, I mean, of the sense of the existence in him of a personal will.

Pilnyak was the victim of a veritable pogrom, a literary lynching at the hands of a mob instigated and egged on by the state power, a hounding and baiting and branding and pounding and menacing on the platform and in the press from one end of the Soviet Union to the other, such as would break down a far more heroic fibre of mind than his. He was moreover in that exigency deserted by his friends like a leper. He had already been brought to his knees once when the storm broke. He threw himself into that position again, and has since knelt weakly hat in hand, begging for the privilege of "violating his talent," begging for the privilege of getting rich writing such poor imitations of Pollyanna ballyhoo as a man with a genius for disorganized rank, sombre realism, and no other genius whatever, can. There is no artistic self-respect left in him. There is no self left in him—except what clings to that small shred of independent volition, that sole pitiable remnant of something not dictated to him by his masters, the *exaggeratedness* of his self-humiliation before them. That, I think, is the explanation of Pilnyak's too frequent and too queerly watery rituals of contrition.

Pilnyak's trouble began with an audacious and somewhat gruesome prank. A story with a mysterious, and so far as mind can fathom it a totally irrelevant title, *The Tale of an Unextinguished Moon*, describes how at the direction of the party executive a military commander was sent to the operating table, against his own will and against the advice of his physicians, and there died. A sinister and tragically morbid atmosphere pervades the tale. The fact is known that Stalin insisted upon putting Frunze, Trotsky's successor at the head of the Red Army, under the knife against his will, and that Frunze died. The incident had been whispered over as an example of Stalin's ruthless taste for dictatorial acts of power. It had, of course, been still more pointedly whispered over by those hating Stalin and thirsting for a sensation. Pilnyak's story was therefore an act of *lèse majesté*. He was in the Far East at the time of its publication and found himself unable to get a visa home. He did not get home until he had publicly "acknowledged his mistake," disavowing *The Tale of an Unextinguished Moon* as politically harmful.

That was, however, merely a foretaste of the castigation and the mental tragedy to come. Pilnyak's genius for writing beautifully awful stories might have been kept within bounds thenceforward by a watchful sentry on the "publishing front." But Pilnyak is afflicted—as you see from the quotation above—with a liquid and almost torrential flow of opinions. A few commas and semicolons here and there is about all that can be done to stem it. This naturally brought him into prominence among those writers—and they were almost all the eminent literary talents in Russia—who, while loyal to the revolution and the soviet state, resisted the whip of the bureaucracy. These writers were organized, as I have said, in that "All Russian Union of Writers," or genuine Authors' League, which stood against the monster-child of Stalinism, Auerbach's RAPP, manfully endeavoring to hold up some last trace or memory of the independent rights of art. Pilnyak became the president of this Authors' League, and the principle focus of its Moscow activities—Eugene Zamyatin occupying a like position in Leningrad. In order to break the resistance of the Authors' League and consolidate the dictatorship of RAPP— the political machine control, that is, of all literary expression in the Soviet Union—it was necessary to attack and destroy these two outstanding novelists, frighten and stampede their followers into repudiating them, and in that blaze of rage and terror known in Russia by the inimitable adjective "pogromny," get the whole administration of the League recalled and a new crowd supplied by Auerbach elected in their place.

The frame-up was as flagrantly false, as deliberately devised, as ruthlessly put over, as any in the history of capitalist oppression. Without a word of warning there suddenly appeared in the *Literary Gazette* that leading editorial of which I have already spoken, accusing the two men in one breath of treasonable relations with White Guard circles abroad—"collaboration with émigré Social Revolutionaries," "contact with organizations bitterly hostile to the land of the soviets," were the phrases used

—and summoning "all soviet sociality" to support *The Literary Gazette* in condemning these "completely unpermissible acts."

Volin's charge against Pilnyak was that he wrote a story called *Mahogany*, slandering the soviet system and attacking the socialist construction, that when he offered this for publication in the Soviet Union it was rejected on grounds of political censorship, and that Pilnyak then got into "contact" with "a publisher of the Berlin White Guards," and arranged to have his treasonable novel brought out in a foreign country. I have described the nature and basis of the charge against Zamyatin. The trick played upon Pilnyak was no less foul. The whole proceeding throughout was an exact parallel of the accusation of pro-German conspiracy raised against John Reed, against Eugene Debs, Bill Haywood and others during the World War, except that it was more cold-bloodedly invented and the hysteria against the "public enemy" more artificially stimulated and more perfectly controlled.

You must again remember that Pilnyak has a genius for sombre realism and no other genius at all. To a professional vulgarian demanding Pollyanna ballyhoo in the name of proletarian art, anything Pilnyak wrote would be an "attack" and a "slander" upon anything he wrote about, his heart being dark, his eye harsh, and his art poignant. Otherwise, there is not one honest word, not one word honestly set down, in all this accusation. Its falsity was, in fact, evident on the face of it. You could just as plausibly accuse Pilnyak and Zamyatin of shoving their heads into a buzz-saw as of taking a manuscript refused publication in the Soviet Union on political grounds to counter-revolutionary publications abroad. An accusation of *secret* treasonable relations with a military enemy is plausible. To accuse intelligent and sane men, flourishing prominently in the social life of a community, of entering into such relations for the purpose of *world-wide publication,* is either deliberate lying or damned nonsense, and this was perfectly clear to everyone not too frightened to think. But moreover, the facts in the case were easily accessible to all who wanted them. Pilnyak did not get in contact, after his manuscript was rejected by the soviet publishers, with a foreign White Guard publisher. The manuscript was not rejected by soviet publishers. He did not get in contact with a foreign publisher. The foreign publisher who brought it out had never had anything to do with White Guards, but was the regular Berlin publisher of many eminent soviet writers.

Pilnyak stated these facts in a letter to the editor— the only words ever printed, or that could be printed in Russia, in his defense. I quote the substance of his letter:

"1. The tale 'Mahogany' was finished January 15, 1929. On February 14th I began a novel (now in process of completion) in which *Mahogany* is worked over into chapters. In my writing table there is preserved the manuscript of *Mahogany* with an annotation by one of the editors of *Krassnaia Nov:* 'For printing in No. 3, 23–2–29.' (For the sake of objectivity I must say that *Krassnaia Nov* made some cuts in the tale, but this does not alter the essence of the thing.)

"The tale, *Mahogany*, never having been in the *Glavlit* * failed to appear in the Soviet Union, not because it had been forbidden, but because I decided to make it over. I went to work making it over on February 14th, whereas the above note of the editor bears the date of the 23d.

"2. Nevertheless *Mahogany* appeared as a separate book published by Petropolis, being put on the market in the middle of March.

"I had, along with other Soviet writers, concluded a standard contract with a member of the Collegium of Attorneys of the Leningrad Courts, I. Ya. Rabinovitz, by the terms of which he was to represent my author's rights beyond the borders of the Soviet Union. The aim of the contract was to avoid those disadvantages for Soviet writers due to the absence of literary conventions—by having the productions of Soviet writers appear at least one day earlier abroad than in the Soviet Union. . . . According to this contract I was obliged to send my manuscripts to Leningrad immediately after writing them, so that Rabinovitz could forward them abroad (through the *Leningrad Department of the All-Union Society for Cultural Relations*), where they could appear in print before they appeared in the Soviet Union.

"The manuscript of *Mahogany* was sent by Rab-

* Central Administration of Literary Affairs.

inovitz through the Leningrad Department of the All-Union Society for Cultural Relations. The manuscript was sent by me to Rabinovitz in the 20's of January, and the question whether I should publish *Mahogany*, my plan to work it over, was decided in the 20's of February. I was unable to forewarn Rabinovitz, since my book was already on the market in March. I learned of the fact that *Mahogany* was published by Petropolis only when I received a copy of the book. *Moreover*, in the catalogue of Petropolis—this 'publisher of Berlin White Guards' as Volin describes it—I had read that the books of my comrades in Soviet literature are published there: Andreev, Vera Imber, V. Kaverin, Nikitin, Romanov, Tolstoy, Fedin and others, and I had found not one single name of an émigré author. Subsequent to *Mahogany*, according to information I have received from comrades with authority, the work of Sholokhov, *The Silent Don*, was published by the same house. The list of authors named above did not suggest to me the idea that I had 'come in contact with organizations bitterly hostile to the land of the Soviets.' "

In his editorial launching the frame-up, Volin had cried: "If his novel was printed by émigrés without his knowledge and against his will, why did not Pilnyak, the president of the Russian Union of Writers, protest?"

To this Pilnyak replied that he had protested—where protest was alone called for—in the foreign journals whose reviews had misrepresented his realistic art as an attack on Soviet civilization. He quoted his own letter of protest, which reads in part as follows:

"Not having the leisure to enter a polemic with émigrés, I find it necessary to bring to the attention of readers who respect the destiny of the Soviet Union that: Not in the first place, but in the 10th, and in the 40th—the actuality in Russia is a scraping-off of the past, a scraping-off of the Philistine restorationists, petty thieves, debauchees and loafers, who sometimes raise their heads from under the floor-boards and bedbug cracks. The Soviet Union is strong enough to see, and not to be frightened by, these bedbug cracks, which are being zealously destroyed and toward the destruction *of* which *Mahogany* will be a help. . . .

"Accept, Mr. Editor, the assurance of my respect and my deep conviction that this is the sole course for the Soviet Union and our only road to victory."

After quoting his letter of protest, Pilnyak concludes his letter to the *Literary Gazette* as follows:

"I feel myself to be in an atmosphere of persecution. Under such circumstances it is difficult to defend oneself, and to work is still harder, but nevertheless, being one of the founders of Soviet literature, the first in the RSFSR to publish tales about the Soviet revolution, I wish to and will work only for Soviet literature, for that is the attitude of every honest writer and man."

Again you might think that the editor of a governmental organ in a land which is "building socialism," having accused an innocent man of state treason, would, when the accusation was proven false, retract it. Not so in Stalin's Russia. The frame-up had not been invented for that purpose. The editor replied with louder invective, dismissing Pilnyak's circumstantial letter without shame as a "formal evasion," not answering a word of it, pouncing upon Pilnyak with new snarls and savagery as "an agent of the class enemy," who had made "a decisive break with the social revolution," and changed "from a fellow traveller to a bourgeois writer," whose works were "wholly directed against soviet reality and against the socialist construction." Besides thus sinking his own teeth home, Volin drowned Pilnyak's letter in a solid newspaper page of virulent denunciations from other bureaucrats of Pilnyak's "treason"—among them a letter from the secretariat of RAPP revealing the purpose of the whole frame-up, a summons to the Authors' League, of which Pilnyak was president, to "make the necessary inferences" and convert itself into a "genuine organization of Soviet writers." "We place before the fellow travellers the question sharp and direct: either for Pilnyak and his patrons or against them. There is no third alternative."

If I have conveyed to the reader any idea of the organized violence of this attack, and the ruthless state power known to stand behind it, he will not be surprised to know that the Authors' League—not without dispute, not without courageous voices raised in protest, yet in the end by an overwhelming vote—joined the stampede.

They joined the stampede in terror—in terror for their own right to publication, their bread and butter, their social existence. In the next issue of *The Literary Gazette,* September 9th, the tearing to pieces of Pilnyak occupied all but two whole newspaper pages, or approximately one-half of the contents of this all-powerful journal. And in the midst of this raging sea, or billowing wolf-pack, of abuse and denunciation, appears an announcement of the gradually approaching goal of the whole enterprise, its political objective—a declaration of the Authors' League that "the conduct of Boris Pilnyak is unworthy of the calling of a soviet writer." To these fellow authors who had but recently elevated him to the presidency of their organization, the facts above recited—and absolutely nothing more—seemed adequate, so frightened were they for their own skins, to damn Pilnyak absolutely. Under the headline "Not A Mistake But A Crime," they issued the following proclamation: "The Board of Governors considers it impossible to retain Boris Pilnyak on the staff of the administrative organs of the League, and calls attention to his announced resignation from its administrative staff."

The rest of the first page and a half of the paper is filled with ritual excoriations of Pilnyak and Zamyatin from literary and artistic organizations in every corner of the Soviet Union. These "monolithic" denunciations —ordered from Moscow by telegram, and forwarded automatically by well-trained officials who have extracted a "unanimous vote" from a handful of mere listeners knowing absolutely nothing and caring less about the facts—have been a regular feature of the Stalin regime ever since their successful employment against Trotsky. What honest men think of them is only expressed through the underground channel of the popular "anecdote"— usually obscene. Some of the headlines of these telegrams and the phrases employed were: "Anti-Soviet Campaign," "Political Perversion," "Pseudo-apolitism," "Fraternization with White Guards," "Conscious Break with Soviet Society," "Political Unprincipledness," "Political Double-dealing," "Shameful Conduct," "Tribunes of the Bourgeoisie," "Traitors to the Revolution," "Literary Sabotage" "Treason at the Front." The editorial in this issue calls upon "all soviet society to fall with all its might upon Pilnyakism, which is eating up like rust the will to socialist construction." And it again reveals the fundamental purpose of the whole frame-up by drawing attention to the fact that Pilnyak is the President, and Zamyatin a recent head of the Leningrad branch of the Authors' League, and by "supporting" RAPP in the demand that the League be cleaned out and reorganized from top to bottom—converted, that is, into a creature of Auerbach and thus of the Infallible Leader himself.

Subsequent issues of *The Literary Gazette* devote from one to two pages to the baiting of Pilnyak—mouthing the same poisonous and false phrases so long as the readers can possibly stand them. And they contain—at last— the announcement that the Authors' League has been reorganized and a new administration "elected" from top to bottom. The destruction of Pilnyak and Zamyatin has, that is to say, achieved its end.

In all this ocean of rage, in which literary humanity is seen yapping and howling and pouncing like a pack of wolves upon a man whom they had themselves chosen as their leader the moment he was stricken down with a cowardly lie, I can find but two words suggesting a courageous thought either of justice or of mercy. One is the following statement from Vsevolod Ivanov: "If the facts affirmed by *The Literary Gazette* should be confirmed, namely, the collaboration of Soviet writers in the émigré press, these facts can not be called anything but foulness and treason and should be called to the immediate attention of the criminal courts of the Soviet Union." While this sounds as ferocious as the rest, it is, to the perceiving mind, a refutation of the charge, for everybody knew that Pilnyak and Zamyatin would not be arraigned before the criminal courts. Everybody knew also that they would be arraigned, if the charge were true. Ivanov added, moreover, that he thought a "mistake" had been made in regard to Pilnyak and Zamyatin. The other courageous statement was from a fellow writer, Zozulia: "The appearance of the book in the White press was obviously due to negligence."

These were the sole just and truthful answers made to a questionnaire sent to Russia's leading writers by *The Literary Gazette,* asking: "What is your answer to the question raised by the Literary Gazette as to the collaboration of Soviet writers in émigré publications?"—everybody fully understanding that there was not, and could not be, such a question—"and as to the acts of Boris Pilnyak and Eugene Zamyatin?" To such a degree were men of art and letters terrorized and trembling in their uniforms under the Literary Inquisition.

The further story of Pilnyak's humiliation I have

from two friends of his, one as well qualified, I judge, as any man besides himself to know the facts. Pilnyak in extreme misery, came to Gronsky, the editor of *Izvestia*, begging him to intercede with the powers, and declaring that if someone did not call off the mad dogs of Auerbach, he would commit suicide. Probably Pilnyak had come as near to the idea of suicide as a person of his easy nature can. Gronsky, at any rate, has boasted privately that he saved Pilnyak from suicide. He assured Pilnyak that although a nation-wide self-repudiation made on his knees with hat in hand would hardly be enough, nevertheless if he would do something affirmative to prove to "soviet sociality" his loyal faith, the storm might yet be calmed. Moreover, he promised to try to get Pilnyak a visa for a journey abroad, where he would be for a time out of the teeth of "soviet sociality" and have an opportunity to draw a quiet breath. Gronsky, according to my informants, then told Pilnyak the story of Professor Poletika, and urged him to rewrite *Mahogany* in the form of propaganda for socialistic construction and the five-year plan.

Pilnyak—once proud to cry, "I very well know that I can not write otherwise than I do write; I am unable to, and will not, even though I should want to violate myself"—trudged humbly down the stairs and home to work on the task of castrating his harsh novel, shaving its hairs off, soaping and dressing it up in the made-to-order clothes of regimental propaganda. In this great work of creative art he was kept enthusiastic by an unremittent persecution in the press. And when the work was done, and the product adorned with a new title, *The Volga*

Falls to the Caspian Sea—one fact, at least, that propaganda can not alter—he took it back to Gronsky, and to his infinite relief it was accepted for publication.

And how about the visa?—he then ventured to ask.

Not yet, my lad!—Gronsky answered. This job was merely to save *you,* just a matter of saving your skin. Now you must render as *unselfish* service to the Soviet Republic.

Gronsky then explained to Pilnyak that Stalin was particularly concerned to establish his success in matters pertaining to the "national problem"—that is, the Bolshevik policy toward minor nationalities, a policy which Lenin had on his deathbed accused him of betraying.

Go into one of our great autonomous republics—Gronsky said to Pilnyak. Travel about and live there for a while. Find out what wonders our leader has performed for the subject races. Write a book about it. Then come back, and if you have done a good job, I will see what I can do about the visa.

So Pilnyak, again swallowing that "law which makes it impossible to violate a literary talent," disappeared into Central Asia. He was back soon with another volume of made-to-order propaganda—a "campaign circular," is what we should call it—entitled *Kadzikistan: Soviet Seventh.* This too was accepted for publication. The campaign of slander did not cease, but it subsided sufficiently to impress the suffering culprit with the might and magnitude of Gronsky's efforts in his behalf.

He again asked timidly about the visa.

Of course! Of course!—said Gronsky. But I wonder what you will use for money abroad? We can not afford the valuta, of course. Surely you wouldn't suggest that we spend on your personal needs money needed for the five-year plan which you yourself have been so enthusiastically extolling?

So Pilnyak trudged down the stairs again—comforting himself, perhaps, with the thought that when an artist does sell out, he gets "gypped." So much, at least, of his proud "literary law" survived.

But here this sad story is illumined by the arrival of a good fairy, a most appropriate good fairy, since the story is of the corruption of a literary artist—the editor, namely, of Hearst's Cosmopolitan Magazine. Only that divine American Providence which watches over artists who "violate their talents" can explain the arrival in Moscow at this critical moment of a Hearst editor in search of a Russian genius to exploit. The cash for Pilnyak's holiday was provided like manna from heaven —a story paid for, an advance made against the Volga novel. Pilnyak, at Gronsky's suggestion, wrote a letter to the Infallible Leader himself: Do you know any reason why I could not be permitted to go abroad? To which the Leader responded: No, I do not. Best wishes.

So it was that Boris Pilnyak, the famous propagandist of the five-year plan and the glories of socialist constructivity, arrived in America and was enthusiastically welcomed by Michael Gold in the *New Masses* as a talented "Soviet writer" who owed his reception in America to the "success of the five-year plan which made America willing to hear what he had to say." He was fêted at a great banquet of American arts and letters, a banquet enlivened by an exchange of compliments between

Dreiser and Sinclair Lewis, a slap in the face and a turning of the other cheek, that will be memorable also in American literary annals. He was piloted across the country in an automobile by that pure but diplomatic priest of Stalinism in the field of culture, Joseph Freeman. And in Hollywood—so great is America's eagerness to hear about the five-year plan—he found Irving Thalberg waiting with a salary of five hundred dollars a week for ten weeks—so the rumor runs, though I have not confirmed it. At any rate, an adequate quantity of the great American balm was spread upon Pilnyak's bleeding wounds, and he drove back to New York with Joe Freeman in his own automobile. The car went with him to Russia, where he wrote an indictment of American capitalism under the title, "O.K.," applied for membership in the communist party, and has since been "acknowledging his mistakes" with menstrual regularity and holding his own as "one of the richest men in the Soviet Union."

To crown this story of the humiliation of a great writer, what could be more appropriate than the rapturous remarks with which Michael Gold explained him to the American public?

"Pilnyak, moved by the great crusade of reconstruction and mass culture that attended the five-year plan, went forth with a high seriousness, honesty and passion to observe this crusade and to write about it. . . . It was to be a labor of devotion such as most Soviet writers now contribute to the revolution. . . . Pilnyak must have sat down to write the

epic of rivers and dams in a heroic mood. . . .
The artistic conscience of Russian writers today is
haunted by such epic necessities."

According to this "Marxian critic" Pilnyak failed in
his high and heroic endeavor to obey the dictates of the
"conscience" of the Soviet artist "because he is obsessed
by a bookish nostalgia for feudalism" and is "an industrialist who fears the socialization of the intellectual
monopoly."

Pilnyak is not an industrialist, and he has no yearning
for feudalism. He is loyal to the revolution and the Soviet
system, and has been crippled as an artist by being beaten
half to death with the club of the Stalin bureaucracy.
Probably no work of art in the world's history was ever
completed in more direct violation of the artist's conscience, or with a more unadulterated motive of self-
preservation than Pilnyak's *The Volga Falls to the
Caspian Sea.*

CHAPTER XII

TROTSKY SPEAKS FOR ART'S OWN LAWS

WHAT WE HAVE SEEN UNDER ATTACK FROM THE MACHINE politicians of Stalin, was in no case anti-communist or anti-Soviet propaganda. Such propaganda is suppressed and punished by law. The slightest hint or glimmer of artistic independence, of some strong native way of seeing or creating—a way of seeing or creating distinct from that dictated by the temporary expediencies of the political power—was the object of this extra-legal attack, and was the thing destroyed. It was not a revolutionary power stamping out the counter-revolution. It was bigotry and bureaucracy stamping out creative life.

If any doubts remain about this, they will disappear when we pass from the field of poetic to that of critical literature. For here the conflict becomes completely articulate. Here the thing attacked by the politicians, and wiped out so that no effective trace of it remained in the Soviet Union, was the *opinion* that art has some function independent of practical propaganda.

"The agents of the class enemy," shouts the *Literary Gazette* in giant letters, "are disguising themselves with the fig-leaf of apolitism, with the slogan of the neutrality of art. The task of soviet literary sociality is to expose ruthlessly all neutralism, all apolitism in its midst. We must have a strict Bolshevik vigilance on the publishing front."

And this program of Calvinism—separated by four hundred years of evolution from Lenin's quiet thought: "We need the theatre not so much for propaganda as to rest hard workers after their daily work. . . . We must preserve the beautiful. . . . There is nothing better than the *Appassionata* . . . the proletarian culture must appear as a natural development. . . . Every artist, everybody who wishes to, can claim the right to create freely according to his ideal"—this program was carried out with all the ferocity of the Church's Inquisition, less only the faggot-pile and whipping-post.

Pereversev was perhaps the most gifted and popular teacher of Marxism that Russia possessed. His authority among the young and his influence in support of the soviets, the party and the principles of Bolshevism, were outstanding. But Pereversev loved literature as an art, and moreover had thought deeply about the relations between art and science—as deeply, perhaps, as any orthodox Marxian could. Science, he said, is a "form of human consciousness sharply distinguished in its content from that of art." And introducing his essays upon Dostoyevsky, he said: "I do not intend to seek in Dostoyevsky's works a world philosophy, or political or religious views, because to seek that in an artist is like asking shoes from a baker. The artist creates life, and not systems. He does not reason and does not argue, but lives, imagining himself to be this or that character in this or that situation. . . ." For these outrageous opinions Pereversev was attacked by the At-Your-Postites and

literally, in so far as language in all the authoritary pub-
lications of an entire nation could do it, boiled in oil.
From being the most popular and influential teacher of
Marxism to the young, a professor in the Communist
Academy, he was reduced in less than six months to an
Ishmael of Marxism.

A similar thing happened to Gorbachev, another fine
and thoughtful critic, bold enough to defend "the freedom of creative views within a proletarian literature."

But here again I must desist from piling up a list of
foreign names. My promise was to cite the example of the
two or three indubitable leaders in each broad field of
literary art. And in the field of criticism the indubitable
leaders are Trotsky and Voronsky and Polonsky. The
chief of these, no doubt, is Leon Trotsky, whose *History
of the Russian Revolution* (written, by no accident, in
exile) is the only Russian prose work of the decade which
lays a sure claim to immortality, and whose critical essays
collected in the famous little book *Literature and Revolution* form the very axis of the story we are telling.

It is impossible to understand any important phenomenon in the intellectual history of Russia for the
past ten years, without reference to the campaign to put
down, and *hold down,* "Trotskyism." Since Trotsky rep-
resents, in all essentials, merely a more intelligent, more
instructed, more resolute, more honest and drastic application of the principles upon which Stalin professes to be
acting, the effect of this campaign in the world of ideas
is peculiar. Every wise thing that Trotsky says must be

discredited, either by falsification or flat contradiction. And since Trotsky has a habit of saying wise things right along, official Russian opinion is in a perpetual quandary between falsification and folly. In this matter of proletarian literature it was compelled to choose folly, because Trotsky's point-of-view—essentially supported by Lenin —was published in the party organ *Pravda* early in 1923, and had gained currency before Stalin got his grip upon the press.

It is in *Literature and Revolution* that Trotsky said: Art has its own laws . . . "the Marxian methods are not the same as the artistic." And that deep pronouncement which Auerbach so solemnly dictated to the International Union of Proletarian Writers, "the method of artistic creation is the method of dialectic materialism," was merely the automatic official contradiction of whatever Trotsky had happened to say. The discovery that in this case the contradiction was entirely fatuous, and "said very little" and meant less, required only two years and three months of reflection, which is a short period compared to what has happened in the economic and political fields.

"Art," Trotsky says, "must make its own way and by its own means. . . . The party leads the proletariat, but not the basic processes of history. There are domains in which the party leads, directly and imperatively. There are domains in which it only cooperates. There are, finally, domains in which it only orientates itself. The domain of art is not one in which the party is called upon to command. It can and must protect and help, but it can only lead indirectly. . . .

"Does not such a policy mean, however, that the party is going to have an unprotected flank on the side of art? This is a great exaggeration. The party will repel any clearly poisonous, disintegrating tendencies in art. . . . If the revolution has the right to destroy bridges and monuments whenever necessary, it will stop still less from laying its hand on any tendency in art which, no matter how great its achievement in form, threatens to disintegrate the revolutionary environment or to arouse the internal forces of the revolution, that is, the proletariat, the peasantry and the intelligentsia, to a hostile opposition to one another. Our standard is, clearly, political, imperative and intolerant. But for this very reason, it must define the limits of its activity clearly. For a more precise expression of my meaning, I will say: we ought to have a watchful revolutionary censorship, and a broad and flexible policy in the field of art, free from petty partisan maliciousness."

We breathe here in a different world from that occupied by Stalin's artists in uniform. And if we pursue the thought of Trotsky further, the differences multiply. Even that motto of the John Reed Clubs, "Art is a class weapon," turns out to be a mere manikin's contradiction of something Trotsky said.

If you really believe in the Marxian schema for the

future, Trotsky argued, and in the Bolshevik assumption that the world-wide revolution is now on, the problem of producing a "proletarian culture" does not arise. "History shows that the formation of a new culture which centers around a ruling class demands considerable time and reaches completion only at the period preceding the political decadence of that class. . . . When we wish to denounce any too optimistic views about the transition to socialism, we point out that the period of social revolution on a world scale will occupy not months, not years, but decades—decades but not centuries, certainly not thousands of years. Can the proletariat in this time create a new culture? It is legitimate to doubt this. . . . The energy of the proletariat will be spent mainly in conquering power, in retaining and strengthening it, and in applying it to the most urgent needs of existence and of further struggle. . . . On the other hand, as the new regime becomes more and more protected from political and military surprises and as conditions become more favorable for cultural creation, the proletariat will be more and more dissolved into a socialist community and will free itself from its class characteristics and thus cease to be a proletariat. . . . This seems to lead to the conclusion that there is no proletarian culture and that there never will be any, and in fact there is no reason to regret this. The proletariat acquires power for the purpose of doing away forever with class culture and to make way for human culture. . . .*

* It is well to remember that Trotsky is here expressing an opinion already familiar to revolutionary Marxians in the writings of Rosa Luxemburg. The whole problem about proletarian culture is treated

"At present, in these years of respite, some illusions may arise in our Soviet Republic as regards this. We have put the cultural questions on the order of the day. . . . But no matter how important and vitally necessary our culture-building may be, it is entirely dominated by the approach of European and world revolution. We are, as before, merely soldiers in a campaign. We are bivouacking for a day. Our shirt has to be washed, our hair has to be cut and combed and, most important of all, the rifle has to be cleaned and oiled. Our entire present-day economic and cultural work is nothing more than a bringing of ourselves into order between two battles and two campaigns."

It is clear that these views rest in a conception of artistic culture directly opposed to that which is now being assiduously piped through the world from Moscow. They rest also, no doubt, in a different conception of the revolution. Stalin does not think we are merely bivouacking for the day; he does not wish to press on with the world movement; his policy is to relax the revolutionary struggle elsewhere and "build socialism" in Russia alone. But he and his "theoreticians" do not oppose Trotsky solely, or even primarily, on this ground. They oppose his very conception of the nature of a culture and creative art.

"Trotsky said that the proletariat can not create its own art because it has to keep its weapons cleaned, did he?"

by her in a similar vein, and the conclusion reached that, "The working class can not create its own art and science until after it is completely emancipated from its position as an actual class." (*Vorwaerts*, March 14, 1903.)

"Very well. *Art is a class weapon!*"

That is the type of reasoning by which this famous motto of the John Reed Clubs was arrived at. And without understanding to what an extent that type of reasoning dominates the intellectual atmosphere in Soviet Russia, it is impossible to understand anything at all in the matter we are discussing. The raging zeal, as for a divine decree, with which a false and humiliating view of artistic culture, humiliating not to artists only but to the human race, has been spread through Russia and is on its way round the world, only begins to be intelligible when you know that Russia has been for ten years intermittently in the grip of an anti-Trotskyist hysteria kept up by a press campaign similar to that which swept us into the World War.

That, however, is merely a first step towards understanding this phenomenon. It is not only to contradict what Trotsky said, and declare it "anti-proletarian," that this poetic goose-step has been introduced. For that purpose it would be, of course, sufficient to present Trotsky's rejection of the slogan "proletarian culture" as another example of the celebrated "defeatism" of the victor of the revolutionary wars. Another purpose is served by declaring art identical with party propaganda. It is by this means that in the field of critical and poetic literature, and what we may describe as general speculation, every manifestation of independent intelligent truth-telling about the existing situation—that is, of "Trotskyism"—has been beaten down, or boycotted, or ostracized, or forcibly excluded from the view. The decree that *proletarian art is communist propaganda*, an affront to any

— 133 —

thoughtful man's good sense, is merely the political whip-lash with which poetic heretics and dissenters to Stalin's boss-ship have been driven into the corral or driven out of public life. We need not be surprised to find a similar weapon in the hands of Hitler's minister and Mussolini. Surprising if we never find it nearer home.

A relaxation of concrete purpose is normally accompanied by an increased bigotry of abstract opinion. The task of organizing this bigotry in the sphere of arts and letters when Lenin's thinking yielded place to Stalin's power, was fulfilled in the main by the *At-Your-Post* group, the *Napostovtzi,* who assembled with the conscious purpose of opposing "Trotskyism" in this sphere. Under the leadership, first of Lelevich, then of Auerbach, both past-masters in the truly creative art of identitifying "proletarian culture" with political machine loyalty, this organization carried the doctrine of the "class-essence" of man and "all history," and of "class-differentiation among the fellow travellers," "class vigilance on the publishing front," "class hegemony in creative art," and—in plainer terms—*"seizure of power in literature,"* to such lengths that, what with poets' suicides and silences of prose artists, it began to appear plausible that soon nothing *would* be left of proletarian literature but the straight and careful party stuff, the tracts and homiletic hero stories, and publicity for socialist construction, and for regularity and party discipline and Stalin, sanctioned by this group. I do not mean to say that there were no creative talents here. Libedinsky, the gifted author of *A Week,* has always been a foremost member of the *Napostovtzi*. Even Sosnovsky, whom I described as the one eminent literary mind to stand firm against the bureaucratic degeneration, voted with this group in 1924—which shows that almost no one in that period of fever in the literary super-structure, realized what forces in the economic and political foundation were in play. The question: "Are you for the hegemony of the proletariat in literature?" was presented point-blank, like the question: "Has your mother shed her fur?" and an unhesitating answer demanded, *yes* or *no*.

Witch-burning, however, even with full support from the government, tends to run into a kind of undiscriminating inebriation alarming even to those who profit by it. The principle proclaimed by the At-Your-Postites that "things having no political setting and at first glance politically harmless, sometimes turn out to be characteristic productions of the New Bourgeoisie, reflecting the essence of those moods which this group is trying to arouse against the working class"—constructive treason, so to speak, by lyric intimation—made all sober Bolsheviks uneasy. I was reminded of this when I read Diego Rivera's statement that even a painting of a loaf of bread by Cezanne could "reflect the character of the revolutionary artist." If Rivera will imagine a dictatorial power excommunicating and destroying artists on the ground that their loaves of bread do *not* reflect the character of the revolutionary artist, he will know to what inanities of cruel persecution such innocently pleasant dictums lend their aid.

The situation grew so flagrant that a special conference was summoned in the spring of 1924 by the Press Commission of the Central Committee of the party, to thresh out this question about art and culture to the bottom. The At-Your-Postites, drunk with the power their acrid struggle against Trotskyism was already winning them, went before this commission with the demand that their creature, RAPP, be acknowledged the sole authentically "proletarian" group, and formally confirmed in the monopoly on which they had their hands. But Lenin's views were still too fresh in memory; there were still too many of the thinking Bolsheviks in positions of authority. The wise words spoken at that conference were many and impressive, and its decisions, had they been enacted, might have changed our story greatly.

It was remembered there how close had Lenin stood to Trotsky on the theme of art and culture. Both had denounced this light nut's chatter about building a "proletarian culture," as though it could be done by word-of-order from an office-boss. Both had opposed it with the view that proletarian culture means the education of the toiling masses.

"Such terms," says Trotsky, "as 'proletarian literature' and 'proletarian culture' are dangerous, because they erroneously compress the culture of the future into the narrow limits of the present day. They falsify perspectives, they violate proportions, they distort standards and they cultivate the arrogance of small circles, which is most dangerous. . . . The Proletcult means to work for proletarian culture, that is, to struggle obstinately to raise the cultural level of the working class."

And Lenin says: "Proletarian culture . . . is not a thought-up scheme of some people who call themselves specialists in proletarian culture. That is all nonsense. The proletarian culture must appear as a natural development. . . . While we are blabbing about proletarian culture and about its relation with the bourgeois culture, facts have been presented us with figures demonstrating that even in the matter of bourgeois culture things with us are weak indeed. It became known that, as we should have expected, we are still far behind the goal of universal literacy and even our progress in comparison with tzarist times (1897) has been too slow. This will serve as a warning threat and rebuke to those who have been soaring and are soaring in the empyrean of 'proletarian culture.' This shows how much real dirty work remains for us to do in order to attain the level of an ordinary civilized state of western Europe. This shows, moreover, what a minimum of work stands before us now before, on the basis of our proletarian acquisitions, we shall attain any kind of real cultural level at all."

If there is any difference between Lenin's view and Trotsky's, besides the superior intensity of Lenin, it is to be found, I think, only in Trotsky's explicit negative statement: "There is no proletarian culture and there never will be"—a statement which he proceeded to qualify sufficiently to arrive at an affirmative program identical with Lenin's. We have, to be sure, the authority of F. M. Frunze, who succeeded Trotsky at the head of the Red Army, for the assertion that Lenin, too, rejected the very program of a "proletarian culture."

"I must in turn ratify," said Frunze, "what Bukharin has said to you here in regard to the views of Lenin upon this question. In that direction there can be no doubt. Lenin expressed himself decisively against the theory of proletarian culture as a practical task of the present day." *

This, however, may be merely a form of recollection. In his own writings Lenin never laid down this brilliant dictum of negation, which is all that communists are now permitted to remember out of Trotsky's book. In a draft-resolution composed by him for the All Russian Congress of Proletarian Culture in 1920, Lenin emphasized, as Trotsky does, the non-class character of the goal toward which all Soviet cultural work, and all work in the sphere of art, should be moving. But he did not offer a sharp Marxian scheme of development excluding a period of cultural work and artistic production which may be called proletarian.

"In the Soviet worker and peasant republic," he said, "the whole set-up of education, both in the political enlightenment sphere in general, and in the sphere of art especially, ought to be imbued with the spirit of the class struggle of the proletariat for the successful realization of the aims of its dictatorship—that is, the overthrow of the bourgeoisie, the abolition of classes, the end of all exploitation of man by man."

The difference is, it seems to me, that Lenin's conception is more fluid. It does not chop things apart with an axe-blade of logic. I remember reading how in the old *Iskra* days, Lenin asked Trotsky *not* to see Plekhanov about some ticklish question, but let Martov do it. "You

* Spoken at a subsequent conference (1925) and published in Nos. 5 and 6 of the magazine *"At the Literary Post."*

will start chopping," he said. And this chopping is not only false to the historic process, and neglectful of the limits of human knowledge; it is unsympathetic to those engaged enthusiastically in efforts which they call by the name of "proletarian culture," "proletarian art and literature." Here again Lenin is a political leader of consummate subtlety; Trotsky is a brilliant thinker, writer —and commander. Otherwise their views about culture and the revolution are practically identical.

It was largely this fact, I suppose, which led the conference called by the party authorities in 1924 to reject the pretensions of the At-Your-Postites flatly, and rebuke them. One of the high points of the conference was the speech of Nicolai Bukharin, who agrees with Trotsky's views expressed in *Literature and Revolution,* but avoids an attitude of negation by extending the period of the proletarian dictatorship sufficiently to allow a corresponding culture to evolve. Neither of them, it must be said, *knows* the duration of this period. We have again an uncertain factor and a quantitative conception. *Some* proletarian culture was in fact evolving in their talk. Therefore Bukharin's attitude was wiser, and it permitted him to speak an influential word in this debate.

"It seems to me that the best means of ruining proletarian literature, of which 1 am a partisan, the best possible means of ruining it is to reject the principle of free anarchist competition. . . . If we take our stand for a literature which is to be regulated by the state power and enjoy all kinds of privileges, then there is no doubt that we will put an end to proletarian literature."

Another high point in that conference, especially from
our standpoint, was a statement by Meshcheriakov who
represented the state publishing house. "An investigation
has shown," he said, "that not one of the contemporary
proletarian writers is in demand. We have tried to issue
the productions of various proletarian writers—they are
lying in our store rooms and we sell them literally by
weight for there is no demand for them. The work is a
complete loss. That is what compelled us to stop work
along these lines. What is the cause of the unreadability
of the productions of the 'proletarian writers'? The cause
is that they are isolating themselves from the masses.
What is the cause of this isolation from the masses? Because they write in such a way that the mass understands
nothing of what they write."

When the literature called "proletarian" is identifiable
in the publisher's records by its isolation from the masses
in a workers' republic it might be reasonable to infer
that there is something the matter with the definition of
proletarian literature. The conference did not draw that
inference, but it did adopt a series of decisions reflecting
the genuine wisdom of the old Bolshevik leaders. It declared, of course, that "in a class society there is not and
can not be any neutral art." That proposition, obviously
false to an unconstrained mind, but immediately de-
ducible from the dialectic metaphysics, was agreed to
by all. But the party rejected all the pretensions of the
At-Your-Postites, sharply denounced all forms of "pre-

tentious, semi-literate and self-satisfied combigotry," * declared that the hegemony of the proletariat must be won
in the field of art by superior productions, that there
must be free competition among all groups, and that the
main task in any case is to raise the cultural level of the
masses.

That wise decision of the party was universally ac-
claimed—in this country notably by Joseph Freeman in
his *Voices of October*—as opening a new era in Soviet
literature. And it did open a new era—an era of "pretentious, semi-literate and self-satisfied combigotry" so
far outdoing the previous period that at the end of six
years it had, as Bukharin predicted, practically put an
end to proletarian literature.

In this contrast between pronouncement and practice
we see one of the characteristic features of Stalinism. The
constitutional party organization is assembled and adopts
a wise and far-seeing decision, condemning in no uncertain language the practices of the bureaucracy which assembled it for that purpose. In the shelter of this wise
and far-seeing decision the bureaucracy continues the
condemned practices with a free conscience and rein-
vigorated step. No better proof that the soldier-
propagandist theory of art is primarily an instrument of
bureaucratic regimentation could be asked, than the fact
that after the Central Committee of the party, guided
by what was left of the old Bolshevik thinkers, had

* *Comchvanstvo* is an abbreviation of communist *chvanstvo*, and
chvanstvo means pompous self-important braggadocio, I suppose, rather
than bigotry.

adopted these firm resolutions rejecting the implications of the theory and harshly rebuking its backers, these backers continued in the saddle, and these implications were developed to an extreme at that time unimaginable. The wave of zealotry of course subsided for a moment. The *At Your Post* magazine was renamed *At Your Literary Post,* and the leaders Lelevich and Rodov, stiff-necked enough to insist that this decision was an out-and-out defeat, were replaced by the more supple Auerbach, who saw in this decision what it did become—the legal cover for a Literary Inquisition.

Since the party authorities and most of the inquisitors themselves, after eight years of it, denounced their own regime of "cliquism," "administrative circle exclusiveness," "left vulgarization," "time-serving," "blackmail," "poisoning of the creative atmosphere," etc., in language that I should not wish to surpass, I will not argue this obvious fact. The change of *At Your Post* to *At Your Literary Post,* did not convert bureaucratic policy-spy and sentry duty into literature. It had the opposite effect. The whole regime from 1925 to 1932 is illumined as though by a spot-light in the formula with which, after the decision of April, 1932, *The Literary Gazette* rallied the writers of Russia round the new program, which it described as a "turning point in Soviet literature":

"All literary organizations, all magazines, all publishers, all critics, must firmly acquire this simple truth—that writers ought first of all to write books."

If any reader, therefore, for some reason distrusts my testimony as to the conditions which developed under cover of the party's wise decision of 1924, he has only to remember that there occurred on April 23, 1932, a change officially described as "a turning point in Soviet literature," and the essence of it was that writers at that moment began to "acquire the truth," or were at least advised to, that their primary business was to create books —that literature, in short, is the art of writing, and not of ostracism, pillory and the guillotine.

The book of Joseph Freeman, Joshua Kunitz and Louis Lozowick, *Voices of October,* was published in 1930, at the very height of the Literary Inquisition, when the authentic voices of October were practically reduced to a death-rattle. How much of the important truth was to be found in its suave pages of documentary optimism may be seen in the fact that the regime these authors describe as a budding paradise of proletarian creative life, is now, since the regime ended, conceded by the officials themselves to have been a veritable death-valley desert. In circular No. 2 sent out from Moscow—for "informatory" purposes—to the Writers' International, we read:

"There was a time when it was considered almost unlawful to speak of the factor of literary talent, and only in whispers could anything be said about the form of our work. This atmosphere did not of course promote the development of literary talent. It even (sic!) had a prejudicial effect." *

---

* Quoted by the author of the circular from a speech of Slonimsky, formerly a "fellow traveller," now a member of the "great united front of Soviet writers," at the plenum of the organization bureau of the Association of Soviet Writers. (It is not necessary to take the words literally —they tell enough without that.)

That book, *Voices of October,* with its wonder story by Joseph Freeman of a "tremendous growth" of proletarian literature, "new poems, plays and novels, finely wrought," and everything going fine, and everybody gloriously happy and productive—these are my phrases, not Freeman's—and all because the party decision of 1924 had "stilled the troubled waters of controversy" and diverted energy "from the politics of literature to the creation of literature"—that book appeared at the exact mathematical center of the time now officially conceded to be one in which the political inquisition was so rabid that loyal revolutionists dared not even discuss whether a work of art possessed talent or not, or so much as mention the question of form above a whisper! . . .

Here are Joseph Freeman's words in the passage in question:

> "The diversion of energy from the politics of literature to the creation of literature following the controversy of 1924 has resulted in tremendous growth. The five years that have passed since the party resolution stilled the troubled waters of controversy over the dictatorship of proletarian literature have witnessed new poems, plays and novels, powerful and finely wrought, many of which can be justly called 'proletarian literature' and all of which, in one way or another, reflect the new life ushered in by the revolution."

Freeman is cautious enough to point out that his book applies only to the five years succeeding the party decision of 1924. He reminds us that "soviet life changes rapidly," and says that "the first reports of the operation of the Five Year Plan indicate that a new period of the development of Soviet life has opened, to be followed, it may be assumed, by a new turn in Soviet art and literature."

His caution is not adequate. The above smooth lines were written, according to his own testimony, in the late autumn of 1929, when a few hours' reading of Soviet journals in the public library would have shown him that the most rabid regimentation of arts and letters so far known to history was in full swing. There were no "first reports" about the operation of the five-year plan. There was a Literary Inquisition. And this Inquisition had been developing steadily throughout the five years he treats of—that is, ever since the party decision of 1924. His book professes to "outline the leading tendencies in Soviet literature" during that period, and yet never gives a hint of its growth, or even its existence. Indeed he offers his book expressly as a *refutation* of the opinion, which he quotes from a "liberal New York Weekly," that Russian literature is "limited by a narrow, official communist outlook," that writers there are "denied the freedom of art," that "lyricism is taboo," that the development of talent is "either totally checked or at least arrested."

The bulk of his refutation rests, according to his own acknowledgment, upon the Book of Vyacheslav Polonsky, *Outline of the Literary Movement of the Revolutionary Epoch.* He ignores the fact that Polonsky's book is a devastating attack on that same "narrow official outlook," and that denial of the "freedom of art," which the New York weekly laments. He ignores the whole chapter devoted by Polonsky to proving that the decision of 1924 was not carried out except in words, and altered nothing. He states—on the authority of Polonsky!—that after that decision all was changed. He ignores Polonsky's anxious warning and demonstration that the article of Lenin on *Party Organization and Party Literature* was written under capitalism and tzarism, and was, even so, devoted solely to the question whether *"party literature,"* having been in the previous illegal period free from the control of the party, should in the new legal period come under that control. He quotes the article *without a date,* just as all Polonsky's persecutors did, as though it expressed the views of Lenin about literature in general under a revolutionary government. He ignores—or has not taken the trouble to find out—that those same bigots of the "narrow official outlook," against whom Polonsky's book was but a timely volley of heroic heavy shot, had already, at the date he went to press, "liquidated" Voronsky, and were well on their way toward the "liquidation" of Polonsky.

Let us compare what the two men, Freeman and Polonsky, say on the all-important question of the At-Your-Postites and the party decision of 1924.

Freeman says: "The addition of the word *literary* to the title of the Left Wing's publication was followed by considerable improvement in its contents. In addition, the editors adopted the slogans: Study, Creation, Self-Criticism. While the old editors said, 'No matter if a work is bad, it is our own,' the new editors said, 'Our own, but not bad.' In general, the writers of the Soviet Union . . . accepted the view of the communist party that they must not seek to obtain 'hegemony' through political means, but should stick to business and gain such eminence as they could on the merit of their work."

Polonsky says: "The latest period of activity of the leaders of the journal, *At the Literary Post,* shows that they have forgotten nothing and learned nothing. Those scandalous methods of criticism and unpermissible methods of literary struggle, condemned by the resolution of the Politburo, were reborn in this journal in still more unacceptable form. If in the first period . . . their methods might be—not justified, but explained, by their minority position, so much the less can we justify the unprincipledness and unscrupulousness of the methods inaugurated by the journal, *At the Literary Post.* Unprincipled alliances . . . 180° changes of front, opportunism, cliquism, a low level of literary education combined with bragging insolence and self-advertising, contempt for the genuine interests of proletarian literature, slovenly and at times dishonest polemics . . ." That is enough to show the peculiar manner in which Joseph Freeman's book is "based upon" Polonsky's.

Freeman quotes Lenin: "Every artist . . . can claim the right to create freely according to his ideal, whether it turns out good or not." He gives no intimation that any change was brought in with the Stalin regime, or that this policy was not in process of fulfillment when he went to press. He quotes further:

". . . The independence of the bourgeois author, artist and actress is merely a pretended independence from the money-bag, from bribery, from being kept. We communists expose this hypocrisy; we rip off the false front; but not in order to achieve a classless literature and art (that will be possible only in a communist, classless society). We do this in order to oppose to the seemingly free but actually bourgeois-bound literature a really free literature which is *openly* bound up with the proletariat. That will be a really free literature because not profits or ambition but the idea of Communism and sympathy for the workers will constantly recruit for it more and more forces. . . ."

A really free literature—and men so kept, so bribed, so tied by profit and ambition, or more often by the bare necessity of having a job and bread to eat and a vehicle of publication, that they dared not even "speak of the factor of literary talent," or raise the question of "form" above a whisper! We here contemplate the depth to which religious zealotry, when it is combined with some sort of solid place in life, will reduce a man who pretends to be a critical thinker in the style of Marx.

I do not say that Joseph Freeman has committed any willful false reporting. Far more subtly serious than that —I say that men committed to the defense of the Stalin bureaucracy, men who identify any trenchant criticism of that regime with "counter-revolution" and with an "attack on Soviet Russia," are unable to tell us about Russia what, as scientific minds concerned with the future of American life, we are in duty bound to know.

CHAPTER XIII

VORONSKY'S FIGHT FOR TRUTH

IT WAS IN RESISTANCE TO THE AT-YOUR-POSTITES AND THEIR creature, RAPP, and to this carefully nurtured public hysteria in which the revolutionary passion was converted into a passion of conformity and religious obedience, and hatred of the unconverted replaced the hatred of oppression and exploitation—it was in resistance to this madness that Voronsky and Polonsky proved their mettle.

When men look back from saner heights, the names of these two editor-critics, who were entrusted under Lenin with the task of nourishing a genuine new art of literature in the relative freedom achieved by the revolution, and who did not betray the trust, will stand very high. These men were both handicapped, in my view, by their strict adherence to the dialectic metaphysics. They were compelled, as all orthodox Marxians are, to invent quaint devices of ratiocination in order to make room in a world whose "reality" is "practical action," for the interest which poets have in suspending action and becoming conscious of the being of the world in its impractical variety. Within the limits imposed by their theoretic belief, however, they fought valiantly for the manhood of art against the "mere left childishness," as Voronsky described it, of the soldier-propagandist slogans.

Voronsky, for instance, defended Turgeniev's view that the artist's business is not to preach ideas but to present "the reality of life," and he borrowed from Tolstoy's Anna Karenina the conception of the artist as one who "removes the veils" from things as they are. One of his books is called *The Art of Seeing the World,* and there he describes the poet, with penetration and rare charm, as one who has the gift to "look with simple eyes at the world as though seeing it for the first time." Nevertheless he is unable to state boldly that since we have been born into this world and here we are, it is *worth while* to see it—and see any part of it, if only a puddle of water or a wash-bowl—with fresh eyes, and that therefore certain ranges of art have no reference to a practical effort by class struggle to revolutionize the world. He is compelled to conceive the class program not as a specific purpose but as a general "essence" of man, and so conclude that no artist after all, no matter how "simple" his glance, can see the reality of any object for any instant except with the "selective" vision of his class. And in order to endow the vision of the proletarian artist with a value superior to that of his class enemy, he lugs forward, of course, that antique Marxian argument-in-a-circle which runs as follows: Since reality is an evolution toward communism, the "rising class" which sees it so, has a truer vision than the classes in decline which see it otherwise.

"An artist who knows the class character of art will therefore throw over all contrary theories," concludes Voronsky, "decide to which class his thoughts and feelings belong, and if he is on the side of the proletariat think how he can best 'remove the veils' in the interest of his class."

It was ably argued by another thoughtful critic, P. S. Kogan, that no fundamental disaccord existed between Voronsky and the leaders of the Literary Inquisition. Theoretically there was none, and there could not be, they all being strict adherents of the State Religion. RAPP's trick of calling Voronsky an "idealist" is but one small item in the Stalin policy of brutal and disloyal falsification of his critics' views. Nevertheless, the opposition between Voronsky and the leaders of the Inquisition was absolute—more absolute perhaps than theoretic disagreements can be. For within the limits of the State Religion, Voronsky was defending the right of artists to an independent vision of the world. Creative art, he said, is in its very nature "individual." And he made a distinction between the individualism of the "art epoch of decadence, the decline and decay of bourgeois society" which "recognized nothing but creation for self and out of self," and the individualism of the artist as such, whose creative effort, no matter how many men it serves, is of necessity a lonely act. This was, of course, in its logical meaning a remark quite obvious to common-sense. But in its *political implication,* it was a revolt against the control of the bureaucrat and nothing else. For that slogan, the "collectivization of art," means nothing downright— as I hope the previous pages have made clear—but that artists are to put on uniforms and take orders from a political machine.

It is wasting ink and paper, when the fighting issues

are so clear, to write long dissertations on the theoretic formulæ. Kogan neatly demonstrates how Voronsky merely stressed the "artistic moment," RAPP the "revolutionary content" of a proletarian art. All true enough —and futile talk and foolish. Voronsky was a man of art and not a bell-boy of the politicians—that is where they differed.

Voronsky's "fat journal" was called *Krassnaia Nov,* which means "Red Virgin Soil." Its founding was inspired by Trotsky, and its policy was based upon that concept which he shared with Lenin of the revolutionary power as a gardener rather than a drill-sergeant in the field of art. Even this journal was, however, to many in the party who loved literature, too close to politics. And Voronsky himself, if I remember rightly, participated in an effort made in 1923 by a group of these poetic-minded Bolsheviks, who were hospitable enough to include me in their number, to found a journal which should give even a wider range to literary experimentation. It is interesting, in view of the subsequent canonization of party propaganda as the sole form of revolutionary art, to remember that Demian Byedny, subsequently the poetic staff-officer of the Stalin clique and certainly the most propaganda-hearted of all the poets of this world, was an enthusiastic member of our group. I recall with particular pleasure his enthusiasm over the article I contributed to our first number, a whimsical tale of my arrival in Russia and my first impression of the people, as remote as *Alice in Wonderland* from the problems of a party propaganda. Sosnovsky, the most eminent literary figure in the party press, a master of what we call human interest stories, was also a member of this group. The bureaucracy, however, already then crystallizing under the cunning hand of Stalin, failed to see the utility of our poetic venture. We were too good friends with Trotsky. The funds voted for our sustenance were revoked after the first issue. We little guessed that within two years no printed utterance could appear in Russia, rhymed or reasoned, until it had been filtered to take out the last residual grains of "Trotskyism." Demian Byedny fled to the Stalinist camp, and I am sure he would be shocked to recall how he once patronized "this American Dickens," as he used laughingly to call me—and that is no insult in Russia—who was able, while in full sympathy with the revolution, to see and smile at things from other angles than their communist utility. Sosnovsky went the way of all those Russian Bolsheviks who combine three qualities—honesty absolute, a high intelligence and extreme courage. He languishes with hundreds more of the old fighters for communism in one of Stalin's "isolators" in Siberia, while Stalin tells his public that in five years more we shall arrive in the Cooperative Commonwealth.

Voronsky fought not only for the artist's right to see the world, but for his right to see it variously and coolly, and with emotion "recollected in tranquillity."

"We are one-sided . . ." he cried, "we can not be otherwise in our days, and that is our strength." But that prevents us from standing apart from ourselves and our compositions and viewing them in a

mood of "cold-blooded appraisal." "We are exclusively purposive; our wills, minds, feelings, are
all collected into one, focussed in one; all their
varieties issue with us in the political struggle . . .
the fighter and politician, swallows up the artist in
us. . . . Our party . . . has not yet produced one
great artist."

With these heresies against the church administration
upon his lips, what profit to Voronsky that he adhered to
the religion, cried "We lack the dialectic!" and endeavored to bring his plea for poetry within the sanctions
of a metaphysics for which "reality" itself is "practical action"? Voronsky was beaten down, slandered, vilified,
misquoted and misrepresented, his great prestige, resting
upon party-membership and association with Lenin
since 1904, reduced to vapor and destroyed, his name
and the name of his strong group "Pereval" identified
with counter-revolution, his editorship taken from him,
and his right to defend his views. In 1928 he was expelled from the party as a "Trotskyist" and shipped off to
Siberia. He is now back in Moscow, writing his memoirs,
and spending his rare gift of luminous thinking and
strong prose and subtle criticism in editing editions of
the classics.

A summation from the *Literary Encyclopedia* of
Voronsky's sins of heresy against Marx, will give the
reader one more glimpse of that system of scholastic
logistics—that revival of a mediæval mental barbarism
—which the dialectic metaphysics, with its talk of "essences," has made possible to Stalin's narrow zealots of

subservience. After quoting from Voronsky what I gave above about seeing the world with simple eyes, the excommunication reads:

"Hence follow conclusions directly hostile to the teaching of Marxism that the essence of man is a complex of social relations, and that the whole world exists for him only as the member of a class. . . . A class-being has no need to renounce his essence in order to 'look with simple eyes at the world as though seeing it for the first time.' Not by denying the class envelope, alleged to destroy the world, but through the experience and practice of classes, society moves forward. With Voronsky, however, what becomes of art as an understanding of life in images, an understanding achieved in the interest of one class or another? Art now seems to have another task: 'Art,' he says, 'has always striven and will strive to return, restore, discover the world, beautiful in itself, to give it in the most purified and immediate sensations.' Thus we see that the chief task of art is not to understand the world in the interest of a class, but to 'remove the veils,' 'discover it.' "

And that is the end of Voronsky.

CHAPTER XIV

POLONSKY'S PERSECUTION

POLONSKY'S STORY IS STILL SADDER IN ITS END. HE JOINED the communist party in 1919—the year of hunger and desperate fighting against the White Guards, when Lenin deemed it safe to leave the party doors wide open, for only men ready for martyrdom would enter them. Polonsky found his martyrdom, but not at the hands of the White Guards. He too was appointed in the days of Lenin's influence to cherish with a "fat journal"—for all Russian literary movements must have their fat journals —the natural growth of a new art and poetry. His journal, *Press and Revolution,** was founded soon after Voronsky's *Krassnaia Nov,* and was only second to it in the work of literary gardening. He was also curator of the Moscow Museum of Fine Arts.

Polonsky, too, in my opinion, was hampered by the dialectic metaphysics in his search for the true equilibrium of a revolutionary critic-cherisher of art. He was compelled to think up elaborate ingenuities for escaping from its rigidly practical and, as all practical schemes must be, inherently monotonous conception of reality. In his essay on Lenin, to be found elsewhere in this book,

* The word press in Russian refers to all printed things, and not so exclusively as with us to the newspapers.

you will see how in order to explain, or even admit into his mind, the simple fact that Lenin loved Beethoven and was moved by Sarah Bernhardt's acting, as any man in full possession of fine faculties must be, he has to invent and piece together a totally scholastic rigamarole about the class character of the "perceptive medium." The artist, he has to explain, may be bourgeois, and the work of art also may be "bourgeois," but at the same time the "perceptive medium"—which means Lenin's brain and nervous system—may be "proletarian." By this circuitous process it becomes possible for a dialectic materialist, without relinquishing his antique doctrine of the "class essence" of everybody, to admit the simple fact that works of art, like circus tricks, or tea, or cigarettes, or games of chess, or mother-love, or swimming, swearing, mountain-climbing, laughing at a joke—have values that appeal to human nature as such, and are not related to the class struggle for the seizure of power. Lenin, for example, loved to hunt—a sport of lords and bourgeois gentlemen. He hunted the same animals the tzar did, or their lineal descendants. The animals, you see, were bourgeois, but the shooting medium was proletarian. What dreadful nonsense! And yet Polonsky was destroyed for insisting, even by this circuitous method, upon introducing a contemplation of some honest facts into the "Marxo-Leninist æsthetics."

Here let us read a breezy word from Lenin to Maxim Gorky, which will show what he thought, as a practical man giving advice in a crisis, of the idea of the "class essence" of man with its corollary of the "Bolshevik creative line." He is speaking about science and not art.

But science, in a lesser way, has suffered much as art has under Stalin. Honest men were ditched, and lackeys and fanatics not ashamed to talk of "Marxist medicine" and "Marxist mathematics," put up high above them. Here is Lenin:

"Dear A. M.,

The news that a 'Bolshevik,' even a former one, is treating you by a new method disturbs me a lot. God save us from comrade-doctors in general, and doctor-Bolsheviks in particular! Believe me, in 99 cases out of 100 the comrade-doctors are 'asses,' as one *good* doctor not long ago told me. I assure you that you must be treated *only* by first class celebrities. To try out on yourself the inventions of a Bolshevik is terrible!!"

How different this sounds from those mediæval ratiocinations about the "perceptive medium" with which poor Polonsky endeavored to make it conceivable to the Scribes and Pharisees that Lenin when he went to the theatre liked to see a "first-class celebrity"?

Nevertheless Polonsky struggled heroically, and with a fine clear stubbornness of mind, to hold some genuine thought of art and culture up out of this Stalin swamp. And Polonsky too was attacked by Stalin's adjutant, Auerbach, with his RAPP and MAPP and LAPP, his Russian, his Moscow, his Leningrad, his All-Union Association of Proletarian Writers, which had become little but an All-Union Association of Art-Spies and Political

Dicks and Tattle-Tales. Polonsky too was attacked and falsified and libelled, hammered, haunted, hounded out of office, out of party, out of press, out of all social breathing space, and out of life. I leave to Louis Fischer, who is a staunch supporter of Stalin's regime, the question why Polonsky died. I can not agree that when a man is destroyed by a typhus germ any other "cause of death" can properly be introduced, but as a mode of suggesting the insensate lengths of RAPP's campaigns of persecution this does not pass beyond the facts.

"If RAPP frowned on a writer," he says, "his career was crippled. It persecuted the fellow travellers, or *popuchiki*, with a bitterness and relentlessness which merely indicated that it had no respect for art . . . RAPP drove . . . brilliant literary figures into silence. RAPP critics never cared about artistic quality. They scarcely ever appreciated ability. Their only criterion was politics, and if the novelist deviated a hair's-breadth from the orthodox dotted line, they stamped him a 'counter-revolutionary'—which finished him completely. Hundreds of manuscripts lay unprinted in the state publishing house because RAPP disapproved of their contents and their authors."

"RAPP wished to destroy all that was not 'proletarian literature.' It certainly has plenty of destruction on its conscience. I think it may be blamed for the death of Vyacheslav Polonsky, the most talented and cultured of Soviet critics. whom it expelled from the editorship of Novy Mir and hounded until, sick of heart and pained and worried by the injustice of RAPP's attitude toward him, he became an easy victim to the typhus germ."

CHAPTER XV

THE "REVOLUTION" OF APRIL 23, 1932

THE OCCASION OF THIS OPEN SPEAKING BY LOUIS FISCHER about literary conditions under Stalin's sovereignty, was of course the decision of Stalin himself that these conditions cease. With that eagerness to be bamboozled which has made the literary mind so often a mere noisy toy-pistol in the hands of men of power, Louis Fischer attributes to RAPP itself, or to the under-inquisitor Auerbach, or to God, or Satan, or I know not what mysterious force of evil, these foul and death-deploying conditions he describes. And he relates with fervor how that very incarnation of the force of righteousness, the natural sovereign, the Infallible Leader, Stalin, stepped forth in his own person just in the nick of time and saved the life of Russian literature.

"Now RAPP is no more!" he cries. "Stalin and his highest collaborators have stricken it from the list of the living, and none will miss it."

Does it occur to this critic to ask *why* "Stalin and his highest collaborators"—most admirable description of a proletarian power—waited nine years, waited until Polonsky was dead, Voronsky in the archives, "Pereval" a noble memory, every honest and courageous voice of thinking criticism choked or buried, before they rushed in thus nobly to the rescue of Russian literature? Does it occur to him to ask *from what source* that ignorant nincompoop, that high-school composition-writer, Auerbach, derived the *power* to dominate Russian literature, and destroy its honesty, and remove its organs of manhood, and martyrize its prophets, and drive its poets to self-destruction, and its wise men to death? Not a thought of it!

"The only regret can be," cries Louis Fischer, "that the authorities discovered RAPP's evil influence so late."! . . . And then also, come to remember it, one more slight shadow on our day of joy: Polonsky—poor Polonsky—"died before the victory."!!

Not only does Louis Fischer give all honor and glory to Stalin for saving from the powers of evil—only nine years late—the few shreds he had left alive of honest art in Russia. That is not enough to satisfy his unction. He must also describe this sudden tyrannous act, which without warning dissolved an organization of 3000 hardworking scribes, rendered nugatory and ridiculous some 30,000 of the books they had written, including the encyclopedias, and some 300,000 or 3,000,000 solemn dissertations and printed speeches and decrees and programs and proclamations upon which the whole literary and artistic life and education of the country was proceeding—he must describe this crowning act of despotism, a mere beheading of his own servants after their successful extermination of his enemies, as a "revolution"! Believe it or not, "A Revolution in Revolutionary History" is the title of Louis Fischer's description of this event.

Let us see, then, in his own words what Louis Fischer's idea of a revolution is:

"The day before the decree which ended RAPP's existence, L. Auerbach, its most aggressive leader, spoke in public about his organization's plans for the future. He did not expect the blow. Why did it come so suddenly? Why the liberal move which substituted a non-partisan writers' league for the party's literary dog-in-the-manger? . . . I think the new policy was due directly to the disgust in highest quarters with the crude persecutions of the *poputchiks* by RAPP and with the ugly personal concomitants of such tactics. Literature, and the cinema and theatre too, were paralyzed by the reign of RAPP, and more and more complaints began to reach the Big Nine of the Communist Politburo who, incidentally, are not as well or as quickly informed as they might be.(!)

"But the revolution in the field of Soviet revolutionary literature has a still deeper explanation. There has been, of late, a reaction here against the narrowmindedness of a few Communists who constituted themselves a sort of Soviet Sinai from which they proceed to hand down the laws for all intellectual activities. The privileges granted the intelligentsia in the summer of 1931, and the cessation of intra-party dissension (Stalin is today the undisputed leader) have been followed by a wave of relative tolerance. It really set in last spring after the bad effects of the 'pogrom' against the 'Trotskyist contraband' had worn off."

A revolution, then, for Louis Fischer consists of a sudden feeling of "disgust" in "highest quarters" with the regime which they have been cherishing for a decade. It consists of the fact that at last for some mysterious reason "complaints begin to reach" these "highest quarters" in their isolation from all public information. It consists, finally, of the fact that after the head boss and author of this whole "disgusting" regime has got himself established as "undisputed leader" by means of a successful "pogrom" against his sole courageous critics—a pogrom about which he also, we must suppose, was not "well-informed"—he graciously condescends to "decree" the "disgusting" regime ended, and receive the grateful praise of all decent men who are as innocent of mind as Louis Fischer.

That is what the word revolution has come to.

As to Louis Fischer's touching regret that "the authorities discovered RAPP's evil influence too late," and that "Stalin and his highest collaborators" are "not as well informed as they might be"—to that this fulsome testimony from Auerbach himself, printed in his journal *Na Lit. Postu* in the height of the Literary Inquisition, will form an eloquent reply. (The italics are mine.)

"Dear Comrade Stalin:

The whole party thinks of you at this time as the meritorious leader of the Bolshevik army, as the first of the first of Leninists, as a man who is a genuine professional revolutionary of the proletariat. We working in the sphere of artistic literature, at first glance removed from the sphere of immediate political struggle, past whose eyes many and many a thing must pass without attention—to our general feeling of love, confidence and esteem for you which we share with the whole party, desire to add a feeling of gratitude to you for your advice and directions. *The broad circles of the party do not know about them.* They do not know that your utterances upon questions of *literary politics* are a rare and notable combination of a calculation of the peculiarities of our sphere of work with an accurate and consistent Bolshevik policy. . . ."

I do not mean to pretend that Stalin himself, or his literary viceroy, Yaroslavsky, has any interest in the fine points of modern poetry, proletarian or otherwise, or any taste for disputations about its future. Stalin likes best the old "classical" ballet, toe-dancing, tulle skirts and all, and that is a fair measure of his interest in the new art of the proletariat. He cared little one way or the other about the Marxo-Leninist æsthetics concocted by the *Napostovtzi,* or the pillory and guillotine of lyric art set up by RAPP. That much of truth there is in Louis Fischer's idea that "Stalin and his highest collaborators" were uninformed about "RAPP's evil influence." The truth in Auerbach's contrary statement is that Stalin *used* this monstrous growth of bigotry, this Auerbach, this "Marxo-Leninist" æsthetic Inquisition, to purge the literary world of "Trotskyism," of honest and courageous revolutionary critics. How far it ran beyond that, he cared little, and if someone interceded for its victims who were innocent of "Trotskyism," he was glad to play the patron and protector—as he did on several occasions.* To hold him irresponsible for its excesses, however, or imagine that, while dominating the whole Soviet state, he was uninformed of what was going on in literary politics, is to reduce literature to a triviality that makes the very question not worth raising. It is also grossly to underestimate the masterhood of Stalin in the craft of politics.

Not only is Stalin watchful of the shifts of power in literary circles, but literary circles are never permitted long to keep their minds off Stalin. Every little while it becomes appropriate to publish in the official literary organs references to the guiding wisdom of the Infallible Leader, and on solemn occasions this rises to a veritable ritual of obeisance. I have just quoted an example from the magazine, *At the Literary Post,* on the occasion of Stalin's fiftieth anniversary. On the same occasion, the front page of *The Literary Gazette* carries under a portrait the following, in large letters as though graven on a monument after the man's death:

"To Comrade Stalin, unbending guide of the Leninist, all-Union Communist party, leader and organizer of the all-Union and world proletariat— greetings!"

To which Stalin replies, in equally impressive type:

". . . You need not doubt, Comrades, that I am ready

* Bulgakov, The Moscow Art Theatre, Pilnyak (See p. 123).

in the future as in the past, to give to the cause of the working class, the cause of the proletarian revolution and world communism, all my strength, all my ability, and if need be, all my blood, drop after drop.   "With deep esteem, J. Stalin."

To those interested in moral atmosphere and character, the contrast between this and Lenin's reticence is striking.

"Comrades," said Lenin's wife, at a memorial meeting immediately after his death, "during these days when I have stood by the body of Vladimir Ilych, I have been thinking his whole life over, and this is what I want to say to you. His heart beat with a burning love for all the toilers, all the oppressed. He never said this himself—no, and I should not say it at a less solemn moment."

There is no truth, then, in the myth that literature is so trivial, or Stalin so stupid, that fellow travellers are "persecuted" "with bitterness and relentlessness," "brilliant literary figures" driven into silence, novelists "finished completely" for "deviating a hair's breadth from the orthodox dotted line," and "the most talented and cultured of Soviet critics . . . "hounded" to death, while Stalin remains "not as well or as quickly informed" about it as he might be. There is no truth in that myth at all. Everybody knew about it. Stalin is responsible for the general line, and RAPP's persecutions were an integral part of the general line.

Moreover, so far from constituting a "revolution," or even a fundamental change in the relations between art and practical politics in the Soviet Union, that decree of April 23rd merely emphasized the central feature of it, the arbitrary and absolute domination of creative effort, so far as that is humanly possible, by the inside clique in a bureaucratically organized political machine of power. Not only was RAPP thus summarily "liquidated" and its very vessel of light, Auerbach, torpedoed and sunk without a trace—and that within a mere breathing-space after he had with circumstantial enthusiasm publicly outlined the plans of his organization right up to and including the creation of poetry under the Cooperative Commonwealth. Not only that, but all those sub-prelates and deputy-drill-masters surrounding Auerbach—if any of them showed some faint gleam of will, or character, or loyalty to principle, or even mere physical momentum in the performance of the daily task—were stopped off with a sharp public rebuke and brought quickly to their knees before the throne of power. A dry paragraph inserted in the lower left-hand column of the back page of the "party organ," *Pravda,* sufficed to call attention to the fact that the *Literary Gazette* (central organ of the whole movement for proletarian literature), in endorsing the decree of the Politburo had not endorsed it with sufficient enthusiasm; that the *Nalitposty* (special organ of Auerbach's majority of RAPP) had permitted an issue to elapse after the promulgation of the decree before the decree was published, and had moreover stated that the guilty issue was already on the press when it was not; that "one of the leaders of RAPP" had made a speech in

Leningrad in which the views of the Politburo were not set forth fully and exactly as his own. The next issue of the *Literary Gazette* contained an editorial acknowledging its mistake in endorsing the decree of the Politburo and not endorsing it enthusiastically enough, a formal revocation of that editorial and promise of a new one swallowing not only its words but all its thoughts. It contained a specially inserted announcement from the editors of *Nalitposty* "acknowledging their mistake" in not publishing the decree of the Politburo in the next number succeeding the promulgation of the decree, and also (by implication) their mistake in lying when they said that this number had been already on the press when the decree was promulgated. It contained a specially inserted announcement from Comrade Chumandrin (Leningrad lieutenant of the deposed Auerbach) "acknowledging his mistake" in having made a speech in Leningrad in which the views of the Politburo were not set forth fully and exactly as his own—a recantation described by his more discreet companions as "manly Bolshevik self-criticism." Thus the builders of the new creative art were lashed and brought to heel. Their prestige, their right to publication, their jobs, their bread-and-butter, in the long run their liberty and social existence, depended upon their coming, and coming quickly. . . .

The true character of this order: "Right-face! March!" to the "proletarian" poets is seen in the swift click of the heels and clock-work leg-spring with which it was obeyed. Stalin called off RAPP because he deemed it, for the present, safe to do so. His honest Bolshevik critics

were all jailed, muzzled, mum or underground. Let
Voronsky try to avail himself of this new decree to say a
few words for the true views of Lenin; let Sosnovsky,
from his solitary prison cell, try to creep into print with
one of his classics of revolutionary journalism; let any
daring young student-friend of Trotsky say one clear
word in honest appraisal of Russia's greatest living his-
torian, essayist and literary critic—you will see what
kind of "creative freedom" this is!

Freedom for Andrey Byelie—unrepentant preacher of
a stale mystic salvation, "a chip of the old regime and its
point of view," as Trotsky accurately described him—
freedom for Andrey Byelie to come forward amid the
plaudits of a "great united front of soviet writers," exchange embraces with the zealots of the late "Bolshevik
creative line" and declare that he is prepared to "social-
ize" his skill! Freedom for "the people from literary circles . . . to convince themselves that Byelie is not nearly
as white as some may think." * I am quoting from circular No. 2, informing the International Union of
Proletarian Writers of these blessed events. This circular
informs us in one section of the "sharpening class struggle" in Russia, and in another imparts the joyful news
that "there are no longer any 'fellow travellers.' " It is
again Comrade Huppert who conveys these glad tidings
to the Artists in Uniform: "There are no longer any
fellow travellers, but (apart from isolated outsiders) only
a great united front of soviet writers, willing to partici-
pate creatively in the work of the socialist cultural revolution."

* The man's name anglicized is Andrew White.

The class struggle is sharpening, but all the artists and writers in Russia are on the revolutionary side!

Could it be made more meticulously clear what this latest zigzag means? Having silenced or banished or jailed his Bolshevik critics on the left with the help of an eight-year literary inquisition, Stalin has now opened the floodgates on the right. Having consolidated his dictatorship in the field of arts and letters under the slogan "Bolshevik Creative Line," he tosses into the discard all political standards of judgment whatever, and permits his henchmen to proclaim to the world that all Russian artists are Bolsheviks. A fit prelude to the invitation of Pilsudski, murderer of Polish workers, to review the Red Army!

Sosnovsky is in jail as a counter-revolutionist. Trotsky is banished. Anyone caught reading his books is denounced to the authorities as a "social-fascist." But Andrey Byelie, Alexei Tolstoy—proscribed two years before as "not even a fellow traveller"—are a part of the "great united front of soviet writers." In April "class differentiation among the fellow travellers" is the sole road to socialist literature. In December, although no fellow traveller has repented, or suffered a conversion, or died, or made any change whatever except to put on warm clothes for the winter, "there are no longer any fellow travellers"—or, as Elbert H. Gary used to say, "We are all socialists now!"

In my opinion all those interested, whether in a new literature or a new life, ought to know and understand these facts.

PART III

ART AND THE MARXIAN PHILOSOPHY

CHAPTER I

THE WORD DIALECTIC

IT HAS BEEN IMPOSSIBLE TO TELL THIS SAD STORY OF THE regimentation of the creative spirit in the name of the proletariat without frequent references to the Marxian philosophy of dialectic materialism. And it is impossible fully to appreciate the story, or skillfully to struggle against its repetition in other countries, without understanding that philosophy. Few people on this side of the planet understand it. Its whole context and posture of mind are so foreign to the sceptical and empirical temper of our Anglo-Saxon culture that we find it difficult to imagine, or even to believe when we are told, that it is what it is.

Thus it is winning a foothold here by mere default. Our leftward intellectuals are beginning to let fall the word *dialectic*—the key word in this system—as lightly as though it meant nothing, and entailed nothing, but a belief in change and the possibility of successful revolutions. They have not the slightest idea what the state of mind is which they are helping to propagate by accepting with this numb acquiescence a word so highly charged with meaning. For my part, I think the question about Art and Propaganda, important though it is, is a mere by-issue in the larger question whether Americans are going to conduct their revolutionary efforts in the name of science, or are going to swallow down this romantic German philosophy.

To the Greeks the word dialectic first meant conversation, and when in the time of the sophists argumentative conversation developed into a fashionable parlor game, the rules of this game were also called dialectic. The game consisted of someone's making an assertion, and someone else's trying to lead him into self-contradiction by asking questions to be answered *yes* or *no*. If you have ever played "twenty questions," and played it ardently, you will remember how it leads inevitably to a consideration of the fundamental categories of conception—the ways in which things can be said to "be." This game, I think, would form an excellent introduction to the study of philosophy. At any rate, that similar game of dialectic did introduce the Greeks to the main body of what became philosophy. And if you will imagine a small leisure-class society, just waking up to the joys of unsuperstitious thinking, "going in for" this slightly bold and improper diversion—improper because it was always leading up to irreverent conclusions about gods—and making a steady fad of it, and then imagine some clever persons coming along and writing "scientific" books on it like Sims on Contract Bridge, you will understand how inevitably this happened. For there were earnest people there, of course, like Socrates and Zeno, who loved truth too well to toss her back and forth quite frivolously. They took the fascinating sport of dialectic seriously, insisting that it is the very essence of the method by which a mind arrives at truth.

And then Plato came, with his mature and calmly smiling equilibrium, and without letting fall the playful humor altogether, converted these parlor games into the greatest of all works of intellectual art, his philosophic dialogues. And when he proposed—not without a hint that perhaps those who believe it are a little crazy—his famous doctrine that the general ideas arrived at and defined in this manner are alone real, and that individual things are a mere shadow, he naturally gave the name of *dialectic* to the science which knows and understands all about these ideas in their pure form. It is a science of intellectual conversation or debate, whether with another or within one's own mind, a taking of contrary positions and then slicing off what is false in each, and so arriving at a higher and better formulation—a mode of progress toward the truth by contradiction and reconciliation.

With Aristotle, who brought those Platonic ideas down into the material world, and made them function as a kind of regulating norm for the growth of actual things, the word dialectic took a drop from its exalted position. Aristotle was interested in observing how things do grow. He had therefore a more complete and scientific view than Plato of the method by which a mind arrives at truth. Dialectic thinking seemed merely critical to him, or "tentative," and not concerned with real or philosophic knowing.

In the Dark or Theological Ages, however, when people again believed that with the help of an initial revelation and of Aristotle's rules for thinking, true knowledge could be spun out of man's head by a thought-process, this word regained its high position. It became in fact a name for all those rules of thinking which had come down from Aristotle. But now, although a sense of the importance of *disputation* still remained, the parlor game was well forgotten. The word no longer called to mind, as with Plato and his predecessors, a definite method of mental progress, a zigzag movement of the mind towards true ideas by setting two views against each other, and letting them resolve their differences in a third. It meant simply logic, and was, as Abelard said, "that *doctrina* . . . whose function is to distinguish between every truth and falsity," and which "as leader in all knowledge . . . holds the primacy and rule of all philosophy."

It was man's gradual understanding that real knowledge—the kind of knowledge you can rely on in action—is neither revealed by God, nor spun out of the head by Aristotle's logic, but is come at by observation and experiment, that made possible our modern world. The development of this "scientific" kind of knowledge throughout the last four hundred years has been perhaps the most momentous thing that ever happened, or could be imagined to happen, in the history of human culture. Do not be deceived about this because from time to time a fad arises to be impatient, or "sceptical," of science. Science itself is sceptical, and the high standard set by scientific knowledge is the very thing that makes us impatient of it.

With this moving up of *investigation* into the place of *disputation*, the word dialectic again dropped low, just as it had with Aristotle. It played no part in the minds of Copernicus, Harvey, Galileo, Newton, and it soon fell

— 178 —

out of use entirely except among the churchly and historic-minded. Laplace, Lavoisier, Helmholtz, Maxwell, Mendeliev, Darwin did their work without it. Science never has made use of it in any form. Only once, when Karl Marx came forward with his so-called "scientific socialism," did this word make even an appearance in a position of honor in any significant work laying claim to the title of science. It then turned up, however, in the field of *social science* with a glory round it like that it had possessed in the Middle Ages. In the mind of the orthodox Marxist, dialectic is again the "leader in all knowledge" and "holds the primacy and rule of all philosophy," and of all science too. It is the supreme *organon*, the ultimate height and perfect instrument of understanding, an inherently revolutionary super-science to which all genuinely progressive minds in every field must eventually learn to conform.

How did this peculiar thing happen? And is it really true that a new "method of thinking" has been discovered, better than that upon which all modern science is built, and that this wonderful discovery is now only slowly filtering through the world along with communist propaganda? It is not true, of course. But the fable is believed in by increasing millions, and it is well worth a strenuous mental effort to find out what *is* true, and how this fable came to be mixed up with a socialism which pretends to be, and seems to be, "scientific."

CHAPTER II

THE RELIGIOUS HERITAGE OF SCIENTIFIC SOCIALISM

IN ORDER TO UNDERSTAND THIS RENEWED APOTHEOSIS OF the word dialectic, it is necessary to realize that the whole momentous growth of matter-of-fact knowledge which we call modern science has had to fight its way every step against resistance from people who were not matter-of-fact, and wanted to go on holding to the old emotional "beliefs" which used to stand firm upon the ground of divine revelation and logical "disputation." These over-soulful people have not wanted to deny science or deprive themselves of its benefits, but neither have they wanted to commit themselves to its methods of acquiring knowledge, and above all to the *limitations* of knowledge which those methods imply. They have wanted to use the faculty of ideation not only in order to change real things in an ideal direction, but also in order to make themselves comfortable among things-as-they-are by thinking up ideal ways of conceiving them. Thus while matter-of-fact men—or men in their matter-of-fact moods—have been building science and trying to clarify its principles, other men or moods of men, less based in matter and less bent on fact, have been inventing a variety of complicated intellectual machinery for keeping up the old wish-fulfilling views of the world as a whole, in spite of the disillusioning discoveries of science about each particular part of it. This wish-fulfilling machinery constitutes about one half, I suppose, of what is called modern philosophy. And it constitutes far more than half of what is called German idealistic philosophy. That may be described almost wholesale as a "disguised theology"—a colossally ingenious speculative wizardry by which the old religious attitudes were maintained in the new scientific world. It was so described by Marx himself. And the most ingenious of all these disguised theologians—the "master wizard" as Marx called him—was George Wilhelm Friedrich Hegel, who dominated German intellectual life when Marx was young.

We need not explore all the intricacies of Hegel's wish-fulfilling machinery. It has two essential elements, or rather two legs upon which it stands, and without which it is nothing. One is an absolute conviction as to the notion put forward somewhat tentatively, I think, by Plato, that the veritable realities of this world are ideas and not things. The other is the brilliant device of conceiving these ideas, not as static entities, but as in a state of fluid logical development. Plato had said, you remember, that these real ideas, conceived as changeless, are to be studied and arrived at by a debating, or dialectic, process, a process of affirmation, contradiction and reconciliation of the opposing views. Hegel declared that the ideas are themselves going through this process. This auto-debating, or dialectic unfolding, of an idea is what every reality in this world consists of. And not only every particular reality, but the world as a whole is a Mind engaged in defining its content by affirmation, self-contradiction and reconciliation of the opposites in a higher unity. It is a Divine Mind evolving with logical necessity and with intense, creative emotion like a deadly serious, soulfully important and noble and inexorable parlor game of dialectic toward the goal of "self-realization."

Now if you are going to believe in God in a scientific age, there are decided advantages in believing in this kind of God. It enables you to be almost as "empirical" and hard-headed and unillusioned as the scientists themselves in describing any particular "phase" that this God may have to go through. It enables you to accept, and even carry forward, the discovery of science that the heavens and the earth and everything on the earth have evolved, that all is change, that nothing we care about is eternal. Next to the discovery that the earth is not the center of the heavens, that has been the most upsetting thought to soulful people. It has been the most difficult for the Eternal Being, the Unchanging, the Ancient of Days, to cope with and survive. And I think it is not too much to say that the essential function of Hegel's philosophy, what has made its ingenuity so significant, is that it saves the face of the Deity when confronted by this modern scientific world of flux and universal evolution. It saves the face of the Deity, and it saves the face of pious, conservative, optimistic morality—not shallowly but deeply optimistic morality—and it re-establishes with a cosmic glamour the virtues of a civil and loyally devout submission to the ordered course of things. If all the world, and human history most especially, is the mind of

God moving with logical necessity through a process of affirmation and self-contradiction, and reformulation in a higher unity, toward the truth of His own being—toward that freedom which you feel when you have solved a problem and got all your definitions right—then obviously there is no use rebelling deeply against the world, or making totally disruptive efforts to reform it. The thing is to feel reverent, to feel that you are a part and member of this divine Reasoning Process, this cosmical Debating Society, and go dutifully along with it toward the logically inevitable solution.

It is easy, when you do not believe in any of it at all, to smile at this colossal enterprise of self-deception. But if you leave your smiles outside, and enter into it and see with what staggering sweeps and intricate ingenuities it is bewilderingly constructed, and if you remember too that it flourished a hundred and more years ago when our own great-grandparents were believing in the literal licks of hell's flames up the pants-legs of the sinner, you will not smile too scornfully. Remember, too, that Hegel did not wait for modern science to confront the godhead with this world of flux and universal evolution so well known to us. He got the jump on science. He foresaw this world, and had his mighty and obscure machinery of cosmic casuistics ready for the job of reinstating soulfulness before the scientists themselves quite knew what they were coming to. It is no wonder, then, that Hegel's metaphysics seemed to many Germans ultimate, and had such influence on those who learned it in their youth.

Marx learned this system in his youth, and fervently

believed it all. He believed it, of course, with a "left-ward" tendency, a tendency to emphasize the temporal and historic character of the divine evolution, and the importance of each forward step in the process, each "negation" of the *status quo*—and particularly the one which he felt to be about due in his own time. It requires only a shift of emphasis in Hegel's system to put God on the side of the rebels. But real rebels in the days of science have no use for God. They do not ask assistance from the cosmos, or any soul-upholding conception of it, in their attempt to overthrow a tyrant class. They ask a scientific method for going at it, and the devil take the cosmos. Indeed they see that all godly cosmic systems tend, in the long run, to reconcile men to oppressive conditions by cherishing illusions about the metaphysical status of those conditions. Marx himself formulated this view of religion in one of his early writings. "The abolition of religion as the illusory happiness of the people," he said, "is a demand for their real happiness"—a thought expressed with greater felicity in the I.W.W. song, "There'll be pie in the sky bye and bye." With this feeling in him, it was inevitable that Marx should throw aside Hegel's scheme for reading soul into the universe, and particularly into the bloody pages of human history, and begin talking about the world as ordinary practical-minded people talk. The world is not made out of ideas, he suddenly discovered, and much less ideas evolving with passionate logic in a benign direction. It is made out of things.

Marx was twenty-five when he arrived at this conviction, which all modern radical-minded people start with.

It was then that he denounced Hegel as the "master wizard," denounced his whole system as "drunken speculation," and endorsed the opinion of the German "materialist," Ludwig Feuerbach, that all speculative philosophers are "priests in disguise." Indeed, Marx went further than Feuerbach, who himself softened the hard facts of science with a sort of "anthropological philosophy," or philosophy of human love. Marx renounced all kinds of wish-fulfilling speculation whatsoever, declaring that if you adopt the attitude of a scientific investigator, no philosophy of any kind except a mere "summary" of your findings is either possible or necessary.

"We recognize but one science," he said, "the science of history . . . a history of nature and a history of men. . . . With the presentation of reality, an independent philosophy loses its existence-medium. In its place can appear at the most a summary of the general results abstracted from an investigation of the historical development of men."

Nowhere in literature is there a more wholesale rejection of the very idea of super-scientific knowledge, a more arrant declaration of independence from metaphysical conceptions of the universe, than in Marx's writings from the age of twenty-five to twenty-seven. Nevertheless, when he came to formulate his own views of what science is—a thing he did very sketchily, and that is why there is so much argument about "understanding Marxism"—it appeared that he had really got rid of but one-half of Hegel's machinery of wish-fulfillment, the notion, namely, that reality is made out of ideas. The notion that reality is "dialectic," which was the very king-pin in the whole soulful-consolatory apparatus of the master-wizard, he never did get rid of. Reality is material, he said emphatically, and even human history can be explained in its grand outlines as an evolution of material things. But nevertheless this evolution is proceeding towards humanly ideal ends. "All successive historic conditions are only transitory steps in the endless evolution of human society from the lower to the higher," as Engels put it. And Marx himself spoke of the "higher life-form toward which the existing society strives irresistibly by its own economic development," and declared on this ground that the workers "have no ideal to realize, they have only to release the elements of the new society which the collapsing bourgeois society carries in its womb." This mysteriously "noble" and ascending movement, moreover, is taking place in the very manner proper to an apotheosis of the parlor game of dialectic. It first asserts something and then this something passes over into its opposite, and then by its own "self-active motion," or in other words by a *logical* necessity, it reconciles or "sublates" these opposites in a higher—that is, a more desirable—unity.

CHAPTER III

WHAT DIALECTIC MEANT TO MARX AND LENIN

MODERN MARXISTS WILL HASTEN TO ASSURE YOU THAT THE "triadic" character of the dialectic movement is not essential. And they are quite right. The essential thing is its going "from the lower to the higher"—in the direction, that is, of the Marxist's wish—and its doing this by way of conflict within a self-contradictory "totality." However, it is not difficult to find sufficiently triadic examples in both Marx and Lenin. Wealth, or private property, said Marx, is "the positive side of an antithesis"; "proletariat and wealth are opposites": it lies therefore in the very nature of a dialectic reality that the conflict between these two "opposites" should resolve itself in a successful proletarian revolution in which "the proletariat itself disappears no less than its conditioning opposite, private property."

To declare that "proletariat and wealth are opposites" is such loose thinking that to us it seems obvious the purpose must be other than the definition of fact with a view to verified knowledge. And yet this loose thinking forms the framework into which the wealth of empirical information in *Das Kapital* has to be forced in order to make credible the "historic necessity" of a social revolution. This loose thinking is essential to the belief that reality is dialectic. It will be found *whenever and wherever* a downright attempt is made to explain what that belief is. Even Benedetto Croce, who wants to save all that he possibly can of Hegel's philosophy because he likes it, is compelled to remark this. Hegel made an "essential error," he says, in failing clearly to conceive what he meant by "opposite"—failing, indeed, to distinguish things which are opposite from things which are merely "distinct." "Who could ever persuade himself," he exclaims, "that religion is the not-being of art and that art and religion are two abstractions which possess truth only in philosophy, the synthesis of both; or that the practical spirit is the negation of the theoretical, that representation is the negation of intuition, civil society the negation of the family, and morality the negation of rights; and that all these concepts are unthinkable outside their synthesis—free spirit, thought, state, ethicity—in the same way as being and not being, which are true only in becoming?" Obviously nobody could persuade himself of these fantastic propositions unless he had some reason to do so other than the desire to understand the world. Hegel's reason was that he wished to keep up, in spite of scientific understanding, a certain attitude of feeling toward the world. It was an attitude of action rather than of feeling that Marx and Lenin wished to keep up. But the thinking by which they did so was just as loose, and the lists of "opposites" which they composed just as fantastic as those of Hegel. In fact, they merely added the class struggle—the opposition of "wealth," or bourgeoisie, and proletariat—to the old lists.

Here, for instance, is Lenin's conception of the dia-

lectic, written in his note-book after studying Hegel's
Science of Logic:

> "Dialectic is the study of how there can be and
> are (how there can become) identical opposites—
> under what circumstances they are identical, con-
> verting themselves one into the other—why the
> mind of man ought not to take these opposites for
> dead, stagnant, but for living, conditional, moving
> things converting themselves one into another. . . .
> "The doubleness of the single and the under-
> standing of its contradictory parts . . . is the *es-
> sence* . . . of the dialectic. . . .
> "In mathematics: + and —. Differential and in-
> tegral.
> "In mechanics: action and reaction.
> "In physics: positive and negative electricity.
> "In chemistry: the combining and dissociation
> of atoms.
> "In social science: the class struggle. . . ."

To this list he adds, in some later notes, the distinction
in logic between the particular and the general: "A leaf
of a tree is green; Ivan is a man; Zhuchka is a dog, etc.
Here already (as Hegel's genius observed) is the dialectic; the particular is the general." And in another
place, he calls the progress of the mind "from living contemplation to abstract thought and from this to practice"
a "dialectic path."

The science of psychology, with all its failings, has
done enough for us so that when a man makes in dead

earnest such preposterous assertions as that $+$ and $-$, action and reaction, wealth and proletariat, particular and general, bear the same relation to each other—still more, that wealth and proletariat resolve their opposition in the social revolution with the same "self-active motion" with which a mind resolves in practice the "opposition" between contemplation and abstract thought —we know that he is driven, whether consciously or not, by some motive other than a desire to understand the world. He is not engaged in scientific investigation, but in rationalizing his motives. Just what the motive was, moreover, whose satisfaction gave a color of solid and solemn truth to this loose mixture of remarks, appears in almost every page of Lenin's notes. This, for instance, from the paragraph next following:

"Development is a 'struggle' of opposites. . . . Only [this] conception affords a key to the 'self-movement' of every existent thing; it alone offers a key to 'leaps,' to 'interruptions of continuity,' to 'transformations into the opposite,' to the destruction of the old and the arising of the new."

It is the "leaps," the "interruptions of continuity," the "destruction of the old and the arising of the new"—in short, the social revolution—that Lenin is interested in. And an underlying, always unspoken assumption that the new is going to be what he wants it to be—that the real is in harmony with the human ideal, provided it is *our* ideal—is just as essential to his philosophy as it was to Hegel's. As a philosopher he is using his mind not merely in order to promote the success of his action, but in order to assure himself that his action will succeed.

That this kind of thinking is not science, but is something which the "speculative thinker" *reads into* science was clearly recognized and stated by Hegel. "The speculative science," he said, "does not in the least ignore the empirical facts contained in the several sciences, but recognizes and adopts them. . . . But besides all this, into the categories of science it introduces and gives currency to other categories." Exactly the same thing is true of the Marxian "dialectic philosophy," as you may see in the assertion of Engels, who expounded it, that Marx did not use the dialectic in order to establish any fact, and also that an understanding of the dialectic nature of such a thing as a barley seed does not enable one to raise barley any better than he could if he did not understand it. What makes the Marxian philosophy so much more difficult than the Hegelian to combat, is that while Marx took over from Hegel this conception of a "speculative" or super-scientific mental operation, he thought that he was being purely scientific, and, indeed, *more* purely scientific than anybody else in the field of sociology. All radically thoughtful modern minds well know that this special kind of thinking, lofty and yet loose, which stands above the best efforts of science, and is not used to prove any facts, and gives you a knowledge of the barley seed which has nothing to do with raising barley, is emotional rationalization, and what it introduces into the categories of science and gives currency to, is the wish-fulfillments of the human heart.

Marx—to sum it up—rejected Hegel's divine spiritualization of the world and the historic process; he declared the fundamental reality to be solid, stubborn, unconscious and unconsoling matter. And then he proceeded to read into that matter the very essence of the Divine Spirit as it had been conceived in Hegel's consoling system, its self-active motion by an inherent logical necessity, the necessity with which in a debating mind the conclusion follows from the premise, toward an ideal end. The end was different, and so were the actions and emotions of one who participated in its evolution toward them, but the conception of the universe was essentially the same.

This fact is grossly evident in those *Theses on Feuerbach* where Marx hastily scribbled down his first and only criticism of the materialist philosophy. He had come to this philosophy through Feuerbach, who was himself not too remote from Hegel to talk at times as though man's sense impressions and the material reality of the world were one and the same thing. "Truth, reality, sensibility," Feuerbach cried, "are identical." "Truth is the totality of human life and being." And he added: "Only that is, which is an object of passion." "Not to love and not to be are identical." As Lange says in his *History of Materialism*, "It is only the philosophy of spirit over again that meets us here in the shape of a philosophy of sensibility." That is what any scientific mind would say. But it was not what Marx said. Marx had only one criticism of Feuerbach's "materialism." He wanted to bring into Feuerbach's conception of sense experience as containing the essential reality of the world, that emphasis upon *purposive action* which had made Hegel's ideal world so habitable to him.

"The chief fault of all materialism heretofore (including Feuerbach's)," he said, "is that the object, reality, sensibility, is conceived only under the form of object or of contemplation; not as human-sensible activity, practice, not subjectively."

It was by means of this extremely anthropocentric, if not anthropomorphic, conception that Marx—in his mental youth and just after reading Feuerbach—reconciled his discovery that the world is made out of matter with his Hegelian faith that it is travelling in a humanly desirable direction. Reality itself, he said, is—or at least is by the revolutionists *to be conceived as*—practical human action. This will enable them to adopt the hard-headed, matter-of-fact mood of the British and French materialists without losing that tacit assumption of a benignly evolving universe which is the essential thing in Hegel. It will enable them to oppose Feuerbach's evangel of brotherly love with an evangel of class loyalty and revolutionary action.

Of course, Marx did not dwell on or develop this anthropocentric conception. He never intended his *Theses on Feuerbach* for publication. The essential fact about his philosophy is that he never worked it out or wrote it. He believed, in his mature reflections—and so, for that matter, did Feuerbach—that "the object, reality," the material world, exists independently of human sense-experience. But he never faced the problem of the relation between this material world and our experience of it, the relation between our sense-impressions and that conceptual knowledge of the external world which is based upon them and yet so often denies their validity. He simply put his famous "theses" away in a drawer and "let it go at that." He was not interested in philosophy except to get rid of it. The *Theses* are important, therefore, merely as revealing the step by which Marx arrived at his conviction that a world made out of matter, and of which our mental life is only a "reflection," is nevertheless engaged, as Hegel's mental world was, in realizing our ideals—provided they are communist ideals.

Hegel apotheosized a parlor game, and managed to attach pious emotions and a conservative goal and moral to a God who had nothing better to do than argue with himself about abstract ideas. Marx took the soul out of the whole fabrication, dispelled the pious emotions and replaced the conservative with a revolutionary goal and moral, but left the apotheosis of the parlor game working away just as miraculously, just as super-scientifically, as it had before. Indeed, in his mature reflections, he left it *more* miraculous, for now it is going through the motions of a debating society, obeying all the rules of order and arriving at the logically imposed result, without possessing reason or knowing anything about what it is doing.

"History proceeds in such a way that the end-result always issues from the conflict of many individual wills. . . . We have thus innumerable conflicting forces, an endless group of parallelograms of forces, giving a resultant—the historic event—which may itself again be regarded as the product of a force acting as a whole without consciousness and without will. For that which each individual desires, meets an opposition from every other, and the result is something which nobody desired."

It is in this blind way, according to Engels, that a material world accomplishes that "endless evolutionary progress . . . from the lower to the higher" which is its dialectic essence. And Marx, if you gather the quotations with some care, leaves equally independent of human will or consciousness the "historic necessity" of the dictatorship of the proletariat and its transition to the "society of the free and equal."

"Man makes his own history, but he does not make it out of the whole cloth; he does not make it out of conditions chosen by himself, but out of such as he finds at hand." "It is unnecessary to add that man is not free to choose the forces of production which serve as the foundation of his entire history, for every force of production is an acquired force, the product of former activity. . . . By virtue of the simple fact that every generation finds at hand the forces of production acquired by an earlier generation . . . there arises a connection in human history, and the history of mankind takes form and shape." "I have added as a new contribution the following propositions: 1) that the existence of classes is bound up in certain phases of material production, 2) that the class struggle leads necessarily to the dictatorship of the proletariat, 3) that this dictatorship is but a transition to the abolition of all classes and the creation of a society of the free and equal."

In a preface to the second edition of *Capital,* Marx makes it even more clear that his material world is doing blindly the same thing that Hegel's ideal world did with reason and emotion—fulfilling the wishes of the philosopher. He quotes with approval a critic who describes his method as follows:

"Marx only troubles himself about one thing: to show, by rigid scientific investigation, the necessity of successive determinate orders of social conditions, and to establish, as impartially as possible, the facts that serve him for fundamental starting points. For this it is quite enough if he proves at the same time, both the necessity of the present order of things, and the necessity of another order into which the first must inevitably pass over; and this is all the same, whether men believe or do not believe it, whether they are conscious or unconscious of it. Marx treats the social movement as a process of natural history, governed by laws not only independent of human will, consciousness and intelligence, but rather on the contrary, determining that will, consciousness and intelligence . . ." Upon this Marx remarks, complimenting the author upon his generosity, "What else is he picturing but the dialectic method?" And he adds: "My dialectic method is not only different from the Hegelian, but is its direct opposite. To Hegel . . . 'the Idea' . . . is the demiurgos of the real world, and the real world is only the external, phenomenal form of 'the Idea.' With me, on the contrary, the ideal is nothing else than the material world reflected by the human mind, and translated into the forms of thought."

Reality here, you see, is no longer to be conceived "subjectively" as "practical human-sensible action." Reality is now independent, and the human mind a mere reflection of it. But this independent reality is still behaving in a humanly practical manner. It is still—however "empirical" the proof may profess to be—engaged in achieving the ideals of the all-too-human philosopher.

I give all these quotations because it is a fashion now to try to save Marx's philosophy by complicating the relation between human consciousness and the material evolution of the world as he conceived it—by making him more Hegelian in one sense and less in another. No complications will obscure the fact, for those who examine it from the standpoint of its motive and the mind-set out of which it developed, that dialectic materialism was a half escape, an unsuccessful attempt to escape, from wish-fulfillment metaphysics into the scientific point of view. Far from abandoning "all philosophy" for science, Marx did not even abandon Hegel's philosophy. He merely replaced Hegel's World Spirit with a World Robot who performs to a different purpose, and without demanding social attentions, all the work which the World Spirit was employed to perform.

"Scientific" socialism, then, *in its intellectual form,* is anything but scientific. It is "philosophy" in the very sense that Marx himself denounced philosophy. A revolutionary science would study the material world with a view to changing it according to some practical plan.

Marx studied the world with a view to making himself believe that it is in process of change according to his plan. Since his plan *is* practical, a revolutionary science is contained in his writings, tangled up in and somewhat distorted by an optimistic system of belief. But the belief is super-scientific, metaphysical—religious in the truest sense of the term. It is a scheme for reading the ideal purpose of the communists and their plan for achieving it into the objective facts, so that their account of the changing world and their plans for changing it become one and the same thing. "It is not a question of putting through some utopian system," they cry, "but of taking a conscious part in the process of social transformation which is going on before our very eyes,"—and therefore, —"All our theories are programs of action." Or, as we find it in the words of Lenin: the dialectic philosophy is "deeper and richer" than "objectivism," because it "includes in itself, so to speak, partisanship, obliging a man in every appraisal of events directly, frankly and openly to take his stand with a definite social group."

CHAPTER IV

UTILITIES OF THE DIALECTIC FAITH

TO IDENTIFY THEORETIC KNOWLEDGE-OF-FACT WITH THE program-of-action of a special social group—to regard partisanship as "deeper" than objective investigation—is so exactly *not* the attitude in which science approaches the world, whether it be pure science or applied, that you would hardly expect to find this thought still living in the minds of educated modern men like Lenin and Trotsky. To hold your wish or purpose in suspense while you define existing facts may be said almost to be the essence of what science is. For a practical revolutionist, however, this complicated mental trick has, or at least has had, advantages entirely apart from its wish-fulfillment function. It has inculcated a flexibility of mind, a freedom from fixed concepts in dealing with social phenomena, a habit of constantly recurring to the facts for new starting-points, new slogans, which—foreshadowed in Marx—became in Lenin the basis for the most brilliant political leadership, perhaps, that this world has seen. It inculcated this free and fluid, and nevertheless inflexibly purposive manner of thinking, before it could have been learned from the evolutionary science of social formations and of the human mind.

It is not true, as Marxians assert, that Marx brought

into the social theories of the eighteenth century rationalists the idea of development, and taught them to regard society as a totality and not just a dog-pile of individuals. Both the study of society as an organic whole, and the study of that whole as in a state of evolution, grew up out of the views of the eighteenth-century rationalists, pushed on by the general development of evolutionary science, without the slightest influence from Marx's working-class philosophy of dialectic materialism. It is true, however, that with his metaphysical conception of society and the mind as cooperatively evolving on a dialectic pattern toward the goal he wanted it to reach, Marx anticipated a social engineering attitude, and invented a technique of engineering with class forces, which might have been a very late result of that more purely scientific development. Just as Hegel forestalled the scientists with his conservative metaphysic, so Marx with his revolutionary metaphysic was far ahead of them in the technique of social action. That may give us a tolerant respect for dialectic materialism, and for the whole German romantic movement in philosophy, but it is, of course, no reason for clinging to a system that is unscientific.

There are two other facts, however, which make it hard to escape from Marx's wish-fulfillment system, and yet retain his scientific contribution and hold to his technique of revolution. One is that social science, when it is applied in action on a grand scale, does differ from physical or mechanical or any other kind of engineering in that the scientists themselves are a part of the material they work with, and *what they think about the experiment may affect its result.* That gives to the dialectic myth bound up in scientific socialism a value similar to that at times possessed by the Christian Science myth in the eyes of a neuro-pathologist. True and resolutely practical science does not hesitate on that account, of course, to explode the myth and face the problem that results. It merely finds an obstacle of genuine though limited utility to overcome.

A similar, though still more limited utility, is the emotional ease with which this cosmic objectification of their plans enables the scientific intellectuals, the "professional revolutionists" as Lenin called them, to identify themselves with the spontaneous movement of the working class. The idea that the socialist thinker, who comes almost inevitably from other classes, is merely "bringing the proletariat a consciousness of its own destiny," enables him to avoid a certain appearance of patronizing, or "putting something over on," the proletariat. His theory-program is a mere "mental reflection" of the proletariat's evolutionary position; his own class origin is incidental; the proletariat would, moreover, in the long run evolve its own consciousness and reach its goal without him. He can at best accelerate the inevitable. This nicety of the dialectic conception inculcates a mood of humble cooperativeness in the *intelligentsia* that can hardly be denied a value on occasions. Nevertheless it is just this nicety that Lenin over-stepped so rudely in his book *What To Do*, which laid the foundations for the Bolshevik triumph.

These subtleties of emotional equilibrium are worth nothing in the long run compared to a clear vision of the facts. And the fact is that Marx's dialectic philosophy, with all its wish to be "scientific," and even to out-science the scientists, is a survival of the intellectual machinery with which over-soulful people have kept up in the face of science wish-fulfillment thoughts about the world. It is an elaborate device for reading the plans of the communists into their description of the developing objective facts. The world is on our side, it teaches them. The real and the motion toward our ideal are the same thing. In order to perceive with accuracy, we must conceive with prejudice.

CHAPTER V

THE MARXIAN AESTHETICS

THE INFERENCES FROM SUCH A METAPHYSIC IN THE SPHERE of art and criticism are momentous. And it is because they have not been appreciated by Anglo-Saxon intellectuals that there is no fruitful battle of minds among us upon this question of art and propaganda. In an ably argued essay, for example, Henry Hazlitt complains of a "deplorable mental confusion" in the new Marxist critics, and even suggests that Marx himself would have been distressed by their abuse of Marxian terms.

"A proletarian . . . ," he says, "in Marx's use of the term, is an exploited manual worker, a factory 'hand,' and he remains a proletarian regardless of his political or economic views. A communist, on the other hand, is a person who, regardless of his economic position, holds a certain definite set of opinions. Most of the new 'Marxian' critics use these terms interchangeably, as if they were synonyms, and as a result some very strange things happen. A Harvard graduate like Dos Passos, for example, is hailed as a great 'proletarian' novelist. Still more abusive is the use of 'bourgeois' in a double sense to mean a person of a certain economic status or a non-communist. . . . This emotive use of words is bound to lead to mental confusion. It is impossible to make out, for example, exactly what the new Marxists mean by 'proletarian literature.' Most of them, most of the time, appear to mean a literature *about* proletarians. Some of them, some of the time, seem to mean a literature *by* proletarians. Some of them, part of the time, mean a *communist* or *revolutionary* literature; and a few of them demand nothing less than a combination of all three of these."

This is penetrating talk from the standpoint of Yankee common-sense, and Yankee common-sense just here is right. But it does not penetrate the minds of the Marxists, or have the slightest effect upon them, because it ignores their philosophical belief. It is not true that Marx, or any close disciple of Marx in a strong moment of orthodoxy, would find this use of terms confusing. The Marxist means by communist literature, literature which serves the communist purpose, and by bourgeois literature, literature which hinders it. But since he has read this communist purpose into the objective development of "reality" as its dialectic essence, and together with the purpose the method of proletarian class-struggle and class-triumph by which it is to be achieved, there is in his *conception of the world* no difference between the literature of the class and the literature consecrated to the purpose. Therefore if the difference does arise in the actual world—if Harvard graduates write panegyrics to Lenin and Simon-pure proletarians sing hymns to Al

Smith—that fact is accidental. It has no conceptual status. It is not of the "essence" of reality, and therefore not a part of true knowledge. Not only it *is* not of that essence, but it can not be allowed by a man of strong purpose to become so. For his purpose having been projected into a conception of reality, any fact which casts doubt upon the conception breeds weakness in the purpose. A man who identifies his theoretic knowledge with his program-of-action is compelled to choose between intellectual honesty and moral resolution. He can not have both, for the facts will not conform to his program—no need of the program if they would—and knowledge must conform to the facts.

It is not by accident that believers in animistic religion are casuistical and get fixed habits of hypocrisy; they are logically compelled to it. Only the infidel is honest. And the same thing is true of that dried husk of religion, the philosophy of dialectic materialism. In combining knowledge-of-reality with program-of-action it leaves us the choice between casuistry and irresolution.

As between these two it is perhaps nobler—it is at least inevitable in strong men—to choose casuistry. That is what the communists have chosen. And they have chosen it very conspicuously upon this topic of art and revolution. They declare, for example, that "such a thing as neutral art in a class society does not and can not exist," and that up to the dawn of the classless society all art is and of necessity must be a "class weapon." If this were a sincere opinion, they would gather up all works of bourgeois art, all the weapons of the class enemy, and destroy them. At the very least they would sequester them. Instead of that they confiscate and throw open to the public the private houses in which the bourgeoisie—for some reason, quite unimaginable upon this hypothesis—had themselves sequestered them. They recklessly open fire upon the revolutionary masses with whole arsenals of these class weapons of the enemy, mowing down the most sensitive and intelligent of their own cohorts. In doing so they describe these objects not as class-weapons, but as "treasures of art," and they boast of the liberating power of the revolution which has "given" them to the masses, and denounce the miserly spirit of the bourgeoisie which had locked them up for its own private enjoyment.

How wonderfully obvious is this inconsistency! A fact stares them in the face out of the windows of their own public buildings, out of their own proclamations and their own grandiose acts—the fact, namely, that art is concerned largely and primarily with immediate values of experience, with the values which they are trying to make accessible to all, not with the purpose or the program or the campaign to make them accessible. And the only recognition of this fact is an occasional furtive admission, in some unusually "realistic" document, that the proletariat has to learn "technique," or has to learn about "form," from the artists of the class enemy. No absorption of Marxists in their purpose or their practical campaign could possibly explain this miracle of blindness to plain facts. The miracle is explained by their identification of this *campaign to change reality* with a *knowledge of the nature of reality as in process of change*—a scheme of ratiocination which leaves no place for the perception of such facts. A criticism which fails to penetrate to that conception of reality can never cure their blindness nor have any effect upon their minds.

A person thinking sensibly, or scientifically, would say that since society can be revolutionized only by prosecuting the class struggle, every individual must *for the purpose of the revolution* be regarded as either bourgeois or proletarian. Exceptions might be made even to that, but such would be the general formula. But a person attributing his own aims to the self-active movement of reality, in order to arrive at the same result, has to tell himself that being as such consists of "totalities" progressing toward "higher" totalities by splitting into conflicting parts; that man as such is not a totality, but is a part of the totality called society—"the essence of man," as Marx put it, "is a complex of social relations"—and this social totality is progressing toward a higher totality by splitting into conflicting parts called classes; and that therefore every man is, and everything he does is, *in essence*, either bourgeois or proletarian.

I can but roughly intimate to the uninitiated the inextricable mazes of this new soviet scholasticism, with its accompaniment of Marxolatry and its deification of the true apostles, which has converted modern Russian intellectual life into a veritable mediæval wilderness of barren and unreal conceptual disputation.* Never since

* Perhaps the best evidence of its influence is the fact that even Leon Trotsky, who in general stands head and shoulders out of it in the clear air, thinks that if someone should come along who could "grasp all the new generalizations" of physical science and "introduce

the day of Galileo has the direct, honest, empirical investigation of fact had to stand up against such a barrage-
fire of deductions from sacred state-supported dogma,
as is directed upon it by the scribes and pharisees of
orthodox Marxism in the employ of the Stalin bureaucracy in Soviet Russia. The question whether these comrades of communism have the *purpose* to emancipate
mankind, or merely a private *knowledge of the future
course of history* which warrants their sitting in the seats
of power, will yet become a central theoretical question
for all clear-headed revolutionists. We may leave that to
time. I hope it is obvious already, however, that the
problem we are discussing, the problem of art and revolutionary engineering, can not be solved until this
antique habit of "conceiving reality" as engaged in
achieving your aims, and your organization as an instrument of this humanly practical reality, is cleanly es-
caped from and forgotten. And the way to escape from
it, as I said, is to substitute for such words as "essence"
and "essential" and "in essence," wherever they arise,
the words "for the purpose of the revolution."

them into the dialectic materialist conception of the world"—a typical
work for church doctors—this deed would be a "scientific landmark"
like *The Origin of Species.*

CHAPTER VI

THE SOUL OF MAN UNDER COMMUNISM

IN MY BOOK SETTING FORTH THE UNSCIENTIFIC CHARACTER
of Hegelian Marxism, I asserted that Lenin, in his practical politics and everyday attitude of mind, continually
ignored this metaphysical conception in which he formally believed. He was correctly denounced as a heretic
by the well-trained priests of dialectic materialism, both
revolutionary and reformist, throughout his life. And
his heresy consisted essentially in regarding his purpose
as a purpose rather than the reflection of a dialectic reality, in studying the existing facts as *conditions* which
make its achievement possible rather than as *causes*
which make it inevitable, and in taking generally the
attitude of a scientific engineer rather than a metaphysical midwife of revolution. I cited seven modifica-
tions introduced by Lenin into the Marxian political
system, all evidences of this sceptical independence of
cosmic formulations which characterizes the modern engineering mind—his assertion of the indispensable rôle
of the "professional revolutionist," his rejection of Men-
sheviks and of the "infantile left" on a psychological
rather than a class basis, his greater emphasis upon the
peasants and colonial peoples, the nature of his party and
the role he gave it both in the revolutionary struggle and

the state, his "policy of sharp turns," and his manner of arguing that a nation backward economically could take the lead in a social revolution.

Lenin's attitude toward our problem of proletarian art and literature is an eighth evidence of his independence of the orthodox belief. Without the slightest effort to bring his words into accord with the Marxian theory of art as a mere function of the dialectic evolution of the forces of production, to say nothing of the intellectual fine-spinning with which Plekhanov tried to transform this into a Marxian system of æsthetics, or the juvenile bigotry of the young bureaucrats who were already preparing to transform this into the system of Art by Word-of-Order from the Party Executive—without so much as a how-do-you-do to any of this scholastic and ecclesiological balderdash surrounding and impending on him, Lenin pointed out the simple fact that the aim of the communists being to make life itself accessible to the masses, and art being of the essence of life, they should quit posing and orating about "proletarian art," and educate the masses to a point where they can enjoy art as it exists and know how to perceive it, and then let them proceed with the further joys and emoluments of its creation. I do not think I exaggerate the affirmative aspect of Lenin's views. He formally declared, of course, that "the Weltanschauung of Marxism is a correct expression of the interests, view-point and culture of the revolutionary proletariat," but all his talk and his concrete directives aim, not toward imposing a "correct" *Weltanschauung* upon the masses, but toward giving freedom to their own creative powers—a freedom in which, if it is genuine, they will certainly create as many *Weltanschauungs* as have the bourgeoisie and landlords in the past.

It would be impossible to exaggerate Lenin's disapproval of all the first beginnings of this talk about the collectivization of art, and art as a class weapon, and art as party propaganda, that has been so sedulously piped throughout the world by Stalin's literary hacks and lackeys. That art both as an object and as a creative venture belongs among those riches, locked away by the masters throughout the ages, which he intends to seize and make accessible to all, is the suppressed premise in every fragment on this subject that survives from Lenin. He did not imagine that complete creative freedom will exist before a classless society is attained, but having seized the power, he desired instantly to use it to the extent possible in order to unlock creative and recreative culture to the toiling masses. That is what "proletarian art" meant, fundamentally, to Lenin. And that is what it will mean to any revolutionist for whom the purpose to achieve a free and reasonable society is a purpose rather than a theory of Being.

Indeed, I think such revolutionists will go beyond Lenin on these questions of the future. Among the elements of sheer utopianism perpetuated by the Marxian metaphysics, none is more fantastic than the idea that human nature is a mere function of the evolution of economic forces, an otherwise completely variable factor. Marxism knows nothing of Mendelian laws, of genes and chromosomes, of hereditary and acquired characters, of all that is comprised in Jennings' phrase, "The Biological Basis of Human Nature." Because of this ignorance—inevitable in Marx, a voluntary self-mutilation in his modern zealots—the idea has been engrafted upon the revolutionary science, and is still flourishing, that once industry is socialized, men will automatically become by instinct humble brothers. They will lose their taste for having personality, for dominance, for rabid selfhood, self-expression, "lordlike individualism." They will only ask to merge their egoisms in the juice of the "collective" being.

This brotherly prune-stew conception of the future is not due only to Marx's ignorance of biology. It is due also to the necessity under which Marx labored—since he was presenting a wish-fulfillment metaphysics as objective science—to hush the element of wish contained in it. Marx could not boldly take up, as all anarchists have and Anglo-Saxon socialists too, the question what kind of future world this organized class struggle can be made to give. "Reality is to be conceived as practical action. . . . Social life is practical" was about all that he could say. "The working-class has not to realize an ideal, but only to release the elements of the new society." And Engels could but add: We are going "from the lower to the higher." To ask in a clear, loud voice, "What *is* higher?" would have shattered the whole system. And that question, not being asked by the conscious mind, was answered by the unconscious—was answered, that is, on the model of the bourgeois happy family and in the tradition of the prevailing churchly faith. It is

Christianity, in short, and infant predilections, that have drawn the missing blueprint for this Marxian scheme of revolutionary engineering.

"All the emotions," says Trotsky, "which we revolutionists at the present time feel apprehensive of naming —so much have they been worn thin by hypocrites and vulgarians—such as disinterested friendship, love for one's neighbor, sympathy, will be the mighty ringing chords of Socialist poetry." I, for my part, would give more for one man honest enough to tell me he can not love his neighbor than for a whole regiment sentimental enough to think they do. It is not only biology but Nietzsche with which the Marxian system needs a modern seasoning. It can pick up an epigram, too, on its way west from Oscar Wilde. "The chief advantage that would result from the establishment of Socialism," he exclaims, in his *Soul of Man under Socialism,* "is, undoubtedly, the fact that Socialism would relieve us from that sordid necessity of living for others which, in the present condition of things, presses so hardly upon almost everybody."

There is little, even in the dialectic logic, to foretell a decline of individualism. There is still less in what the worker in revolt against wage-slavery wants. He may well want to lose his sense of personal distinction in the joys of that humane and rational collective where our present bloody competition for a livelihood has ceased. There is nothing to prevent his wanting this, and there will be nothing, let us hope, to stop his having it. He may, however, and he far more often will, want just that sense of "personality," that selfhood, self-expression, individual-

— 213 —

ism, *lordly* individualism, which has been the privilege
of his masters throughout history. Both these human
tendencies will be with us just as long as man is. There
is no magic in a changed industry to change the nature
man inherits. Selective breeding is the sole technique we
have as yet for doing that. We may legitimately hope
that natural selection under a non-competitive system
may in many generations reduce the numbers of the
mercilessly shrewd and cruel, and habit, education and
tradition still more quickly blunt their claws. But we
have no ground to hope, nor can we reasonably wish,
that under any system persons will cease to be born
and grow up harsh-grained and self-assertive, intolerant
of bonds, repelled by the mere thought of universal
brotherhood, and individualistic to the point of hating
all collective effort and emotion. To me it seems that
when men's rivalrous propulsions are cut off from satisfaction in the sphere of acquisition, we shall see a greater,
not a less, growth of self-assertiveness in art. Just here the
Marxist's vision of the future seems both more utopian
and less vitally inspiring than the poet's.

Even if we must get permission from Moscow, let us
at least try to have our revolution *take place* in America,
and then we shall see whether there is not some western
truth in this more western thought.

In so far, at least, as concerns the hope of a great art
in the future, this thought is absolutely vital. "Art," as
Matthew Josephson has been courageous enough to state,
"demands a lonely and personal effort, rather than a
collective one." And because the success of a proletarian
revolution has come to mean a perpetuation of that col-

lectivity-of-the-cup's-dregs which has been the proletariat's lot in history, he feels impelled to add: "I should
like . . . to see all discussions of æsthetic procedure
cease, and the question of whether art is to survive at all
—and how—taken up." If the practical scheme for bringing about a liberation of mankind from slavery to economics had not been identified with the workings of the
cosmos, and this metaphysical operation turned into a
weapon of bureaucratic boss-rule, and the aim thus twice
forgotten, we should look as instinctively as Oscar Wilde
did to that day of liberation, to ensure not only the survival but the flourishing of art—most often lonely and
personal still, but in open meadows and to a height and
quality undreamed of in the old plutocratic hot-beds.

Look at them again, those slogans of the Artists' International:

> Art renounces individualism.
> Art is to be collectivized.
> Art is to be systemized.
> Art is to be organized.
> Art is to be disciplined.
> Art is to be created "under the careful yet firm
> guidance" of a political party.
> Art is to be wielded as a weapon.

Could any set of ideas more neatly summarize the attitude of the vicariously infantile and office-holding bigot
who calls himself the proletariat, not because he feels
with or for the members of the working class, but be-

cause it swells his importance and accords with his intimate knowledge of the nature and purposes of the universe to do so? To an aspiring proletarian, or anyone joining humbly and with clear purpose in the struggle to emancipate the proletariat, art is recreation, venture, life itself, a casting of new lights on life. Art is what the proletarian has taken weapons in his hands to win. So is individuality. Does it never occur to these sergeant-priests of proletarianism that perhaps the toiling masses have had their bellyful in forty thousand years of being "collectivized," of being "systemized," "organized," "disciplined," of doing whatever they do while the sun is in the air and fresh blood in their veins under the "careful yet firm guidance" of some self-important body of functionaries? The purpose of the revolutionary movement was to emancipate the proletariat, and so humanity, from the strait-jacket of class division and class rule. To this end the student who understands it best and the proletarian who feels it most must unite and organize and fight. The chief peril is that this union may not be real, that it may not long survive the victory—that the proletariat may be used in its own revolution as it was in all others to win the power for a new privileged class. No clearer evidence of the presence of that peril could be offered than this hasty grabbing off of the whole domain of the free creative spirit in the name of a political party dominated by its non-proletarian functionary apparatus, and an esoteric theory of the universe incomprehensible to any but highly specialized technicians in the professorship of philosophy.

LENIN'S VIEWS OF ART AND CULTURE

BY VYACHESLAV POLONSKY

(THE AUTHOR OF THIS ESSAY WAS FOUNDER AND EDITOR, IN Lenin's day, of the important Bolshevik journal *Press and Revolution*; he was also Curator of the Moscow Museum of Fine Arts. He is the man Louis Fischer described as "the most talented and cultured of soviet critics" (see page 159) and whose death in the seventh year of Stalin's decade of devastation Mr. Fischer attributes to persecution by RAPP. The *At-Your-Postites*, mentioned herein, were the group who with Stalin's backing dominated RAPP, and may be regarded in the present connection as identical with it. This article contains the substance of the views which Polonsky opposed to those of RAPP and for which, he was "hounded"—according to Louis Fischer—to death. I have translated it, with slight abbreviation, from Polonsky's *Outline of the Literary Movement of the Revolutionary Epoch*, Moscow, 1928.)

1

It is not easy to expound correctly Lenin's opinions about art, literature and culture. Lenin rarely expressed himself circumstantially upon these questions. They stood in the fringes of his attention, although as we shall see he was not indifferent either to literature or art. In our enormous literary heritage from Lenin only four small articles about L. N. Tolstoy are directly devoted to creative literature. Literature is touched upon obliquely in a note on Hertzen, and the article *Party Organization and Party Literature*. Even in his vast correspondence isolated remarks about art and literature are extremely scant. Lenin's consciousness was so occupied with the fundamental problems of the struggle that there remained neither time nor interest for these realms. This is not surprising, if you bear in mind the might with which Lenin's will was concentrated upon the basic problems of the revolution.

We know little of the man Lenin. The gigantic figure of the leader has hidden and obscured in our minds his human, intimate self. His personal life somehow does not exist for us. No one has yet made us feel the whole Lenin, thinker, fighter, man. Certain recollections in our possession nevertheless portray him as a man to whom nothing human was alien. He loved to laugh and sing and have a good time. He loved music—was so strongly worked upon by the exciting influence of sounds that he avoided it. Maxim Gorky in a few brief lines has thrown an amazing light upon the personality of Lenin. Once in Moscow after hearing Beethoven rendered by a great master at the house of some friends, Lenin said:

"I know nothing better than the Appassionata. I could listen to it every day. Amazing, superhuman music. I always think with pride, perhaps a naïve childish pride: Look what miracles human beings can perform!"

Miracles! And what would Bogdanov say from his "universal organization" point of view? * He would answer, I suppose, that this same Appassionata does not in the least degree organize the minds of men in the direction of the collective-labor view-point.

Lenin would shrug his shoulders—"What nonsense!" and continue to listen to the passionate music of a composer whom you could not by any stretch of imagination call proletarian.

"But I can't listen to music very often," Lenin said to Gorky. "It acts on my nerves, makes me want to talk amiable stupidities and stroke the heads of these beings who, living in a filthy hell, can create such beauty. But today you can't stroke anybody on the head—they'll bite

---

* A. A. Bogdanov was an old opponent of Lenin in theoretical questions, Lenin's book *Materialism and Empiro-criticism* having been principally directed against him. Nevertheless he became after the October revolution the founder and first president of an "Institute of Proletarian Culture." His view of the whole problem of culture conflicted with that of Lenin, and he was subsequently removed. His successor was V. Pletnev, also mentioned herein. Bogdanov advanced long before the revolution the idea that art's function is to "organize, not only the ideas of men, their thought and knowledge, but also their feelings and moods." Proletarian art, he defined as art which organizes men's minds in the direction of collective labor, solidarity, and brotherhood in struggle. He declared—without smiling—that most poetry written by proletarians is not proletarian poetry—is in fact neither proletarian nor poetry. This theory of art set the stage for the attempt of RAPP and the At-Your-Postites, to convert Russian intellectual arts and letters into a narrow propaganda controlled from a central office. Bogdanov, however, wanted his "culture" office independent of the political party. For them "collective labor, solidarity and brotherhood in struggle" meant for the most part loyal obedience to the political machine.

off your hand. You've got to pound them on the head, and pound them ruthlessly, although in the ideal we are against every act of violence." *

We find another surprising trait of Lenin in the memoirs of M. Lyadov. Once in 1904 in Geneva, Lyadov relates, he was at the theatre with Lenin and Krupskaia. The play was *The Lady of the Camellias,* a sentimental bourgeois melodrama. But the actress was Sarah Bernhardt—one whose genius even Auerbach would not call proletarian. "Ilych sat in the dark corner of the box," says Lyadov. "When I glanced at him he was furtively wiping his eyes."

Weeping Lenin! What an unusual spectacle! But from this spectacle you must not conclude: Well, here is this iron man, this steely fighter, able to be sentimental and "pour out tears" over a mere fancy, etc. The point is that the actress drew those tears—that is, the artist—and through the medium of art.

From these accidental traits alone, as preserved to us by Lenin's friends, we could draw some inferences about his attitude to art. He loved art and considered it a mighty power. One of the most important elements of imaginative art Lenin described with the word "beautiful." This dubious term of the old æsthetics is now under a shadow. We attribute to it no essential content. But Lenin never set himself the aim to polish accurately and with full adequacy his attitude to art. He took a "current" word which happened to be at hand, and once remarked:

"We are excessive iconoclasts in the matter of paint-

* *Vladimir Lenin* by Maxim Gorky.

ing. We must preserve the beautiful, take it as a model, make it our starting point even though it is 'old.' " *

Also a remark of unusual importance. In Lenin's opinion the old art possesses elements which compel us to preserve it, treasure it, make it the *starting point* for a further development. Only when we draw such inferences from these remarks do we see that behind the accidental words thrown out in passing, there existed in Lenin's mind a concealed system of opinions about art, even though he himself never thought of giving it a symmetrical and logical formulation.

Recognizing the gigantic power of art, Lenin thought that it ought to be an art not for a few, but for all. The enjoyment which he derived from art only again convinced him of the necessity of struggle. The enjoyment experienced by him personally must be made accessible to all humanity till now deprived of these high experiences.

Is this revolutionary conclusion to be found in the system of æsthetics propounded by A . A. Bogdanov? No, it is not. But nevertheless in the psychology of a genuine revolutionist, æsthetic and other similar experiences are the very things that have kindled a feeling of struggle, of protest, of revolutionary determination. Our schematizer from the viewpoint of the "universal organizational science" affirms that bourgeois art organizes the mind toward the individualistic standpoint—that is, in a direction opposing the interests and aims of the proletariat. But genuine revolutionists coming in contact with genuine and lofty art have in practice experienced the op-

* *Memories of Lenin* by Clara Zetkin.

posite thing: bourgeois art has organized their minds in
the very direction of the aims and tasks of the proletariat.
We have then the contrary picture to that presented us
by Bogdanov. The reason is obvious: he forgot *the perceptive medium*. He knew that in art it is possible to find
the reflection of a class psychology, but he forgot that the
medium perceiving this art is also a class medium, and
the perception, in consequence, can play a critical role.
Bogdanov's æsthetics is bad, from the point of view of
Marxism, in that it fails to reckon on the class character
of the perceptive medium. This circumstance has simply
not been noticed by Bogdanov; it has not been noticed,
either, by his involuntary successors, the *At-Your-Post*
group. But surely from the standpoint of a materialistic
æsthetics resting upon the basis, "existence determines
consciousness," not only what the artistic agent wants to
give is important, but also what the spectator takes from
art. Not only in the creation is a class psychology reflected, but also in the contemplation of artistic productions.

2

"Art belongs to the people," said Lenin. "It ought to
extend with deep roots into the very thick of the broad
toiling masses. It ought to be intelligible to these masses
and loved by them. And it ought to unify the feeling,
thought and will of these masses, elevate them. It ought
to arouse and develop artists among them." Such is the
role and problem of art. This is the category of the
"ought." But Lenin, the great realist, always combined

the category of the "ought" with the category of the "existent."

"In order that art may draw near to the people and the people to art, we must in the first place raise the existing level of culture and education." At first glance this might seem a thought in no way unusual. However in this thought is contained, as a plant in the seed, the attitude of Lenin to proletarian culture, and all artistic questions. The problems of art are problems of education. This means: If you want to advance the cause of art, educate yourselves and teach. You want art to be of the whole people—raise the level of elementary knowledge. You want to please humanity with the wonderful creations of art—understand then that so long as humanity in its overwhelming majority is illiterate, lousy, lives the devil knows in what conditions, does not know how to brush its hair or cut its nails, sleeps on the floor, and lacks the means to alter its mode of life, so long your wonderful creations will remain creations for a minority, for a small circle. In other words, your art will not fulfill a millionth part of its destiny. This does not mean, of course, that we must cease to occupy ourselves with art. It means only that we must not occupy ourselves with blabbing about an art of the whole people, about its democratization, and about building a culture, instead of actually elevating the culture we have—that is, teaching arithmetic and writing, trades, sciences, increasing the elementary economic prosperity.

Lenin's adverse attitude to the talk about proletarian culture stood in close relation to his very deep realism which had seen the vanity and futility and sometimes even danger in empty blab and babble.

Lenin also objected when certain philanthropists of art once offered to the broad masses of the toilers a "pageant." That is nothing, Lenin objected, a pageant is a mere diversion. The toiling masses deserve "something bigger than a pageant. They have acquired the right to a genuinely great art." And for Lenin the realistic practical conclusion flowed directly from this proposition: "For that reason we have placed at the head of our list the broadest possible enlightenment and education. That will lay the foundation for a culture—on condition, of course, that the question of bread is solved. On that foundation there ought to grow up a genuinely new great communist art which will create a form corresponding to its content." *

Lenin attributed so great a significance to art that once when a discussion arose as to what should replace religion, destined as it is to vanish from the consciousness of the toiling masses, he remarked that except for the theatre—that is, for art—there is no institution, "not one organ with which we might replace religion." This was related by M. I. Kalinin in his speech at the 5th All-Union Congress of Art Workers on May 25, 1925.

Lenin considered the Great Theatre a relic of the "landlord culture," and once in a terrible time of hunger even raised the question of closing it. But this did not prevent Lenin from giving a correct appraisal even of this relic of the landlord culture. When in the winter of the "bare year 1919" Comrade Galkin raised in the Council

* *Recollections of Lenin* by Clara Zetkin.

of People's Commissars the question of closing the Great Theatre, defending his motion from just that point of view of the uselessness for the proletariat of this "relic of a landlord culture," which was presenting the same old "bourgeois operas" and "nothing for the workers, nothing for the red soldiers," it was Lenin who saved the Great Theatre from being closed.

Just before the voting he tossed out as though in passing a few apparently insignificant phrases, which decided the fate of the art of opera in our country: "It only seems to me," Lenin let fall, "that Comrade Galkin has a somewhat naïve idea of the role and significance of theatres. A theatre is necessary, not so much for propaganda, as to rest hard workers after their daily work. And it is still early to file away in the archives our heritage from bourgeois art. . . ."

The Great Theatre survived.

Here again if we uncover the meaning of his remark, we find threads uniting it with the other opinions of Lenin about art. Art is not *only* propaganda and not only agitation. "Rest"—that means withdrawing a man from certain impressions and transferring him to qualitatively different impressions. The rest which is given by art is, so to speak, condensed, active, distracting the consciousness in a wholly new direction, into another world. It is a form of rest in which the consciousness is refreshed, enlarged and illumined. How often this function of art— one of the most important—is forgotten in our theoretical arguments and our practice! Is not this the reason why our workers' clubs are so rarely visited—because the winged horse of art is here harnessed to the wagon of badly comprehended agitationism? Lenin loved to observe how the workers rest and enjoy themselves. Krupskaia tells about his wanderings among theatrical productions in the workers' clubs of Paris before the war. The popular revolutionary singer, Montague, was then enjoying a great success among the workers. Art was here in contact with the toiling masses. That attracted Lenin. He who could admire a Sonata of Beethoven, and weep tears over the acting of Sarah Bernhardt, listened with admiration to the melodies and words of the simple songs of a street singer. How much more powerful would Beethoven have been, or Sarah Bernhardt, if they in place of Montague had moved and stirred the hearts of the majority of mankind.

3

Lenin's literary tastes are closely bound up with his opinions upon the universal popularity and intelligibility of art. For instance, he did not like the futurists. He did not like the so-called "new" art. He very often spoke with vicious irony of Maiakovsky and other "ists." He considered Maiakovsky's book *150,000,000* "affected and tricky." Why? Lenin himself gave a clear answer: "I did try several times to read Maiakovsky and couldn't get beyond three lines, kept falling asleep."

"Three lines"—that is said for the word's sake, for what does a "line" of Maiakovsky amount to! * But the thought was this: Maiakovsky is hard for the understanding when you read him. "Pushkin I understand and enjoy," Lenin said. "Nekrassov I acknowledge, but Maia-

* Maiakovsky's lines consisted so often of one or two syllables. *Trans.*

kovsky—excuse me, I can't understand him."

How shall we interpret this? Why did Lenin acknowledge Pushkin and not Maiakovsky? It is because Pushkin was of the whole people. With all the loftiness of his supreme art Pushkin is clear, simple, easy to apprehend, alluring, a poet for the majority. But Maiakovsky is the leader of a narrow school, a poet for the few, hard to apprehend, unable to overcome in himself his small-group origin. Hence Maiakovsky's failure to broaden the circle of his readers. When the poet himself appears before an audience, with his imposing presence, his mighty voice and personal charm, the crowds can listen with interest to his concise and unique declamations. In such moments Maiakovsky really can consider himself a people's poet, accessible to the general understanding. But as soon as the rank-and-file reader finds himself tête-à-tête with Maiakovsky's books, with their broken lines, their peculiar rhythm, with all the latest laboratory conquests in verbal instrumentalization, he begins to feel bored. The art of Maiakovsky travels the road of hindered apprehension. That gives away the origin of his poetry among the intelligentsia, its destination for the few. Maiakovsky lacks just the genius to surmount these peculiarities of his art. It was this thought that Lenin expressed. And he expressed it because he had the *audacity* to do so. You couldn't frighten Lenin with the words "left art." The word "left" means good; if you don't like what is "left," that means you are retrograde, reactionary; it means that you don't know anything about art. Certain gentlemen have made clever use of this word "left." Its whole power derives from the fact that in the struggle for the revolution the left flank was always considered more revolutionary. No wonder, therefore, that people try to use this honorific term in order to insure themselves against criticism in general. "Touch us not, we are Lefts!"—although in reality these "lefts" have often been the most genuine rights. A "fetishization" of leftism exists among us, especially among the young.

It takes audacity to smash through this fetishization. Lenin knew no fear and he openly declared: Maiakovsky is hard for the understanding. The banner of "newness" in itself did not bribe him in the least.

"Why must we bow down to the new," said Lenin to Clara Zetkin, "as though to a god whom we must obey simply because he is new?" "That's nonsense, crass nonsense! There is a lot of artistic hypocrisy here, and of course an unconscious respect for artistic modes prevailing in the west. We are good revolutionists, but nevertheless we feel obliged for some reason to prove that we also stand 'at the height of contemporary culture.' I however make bold to declare myself a 'barbarian.' I am unable to consider the productions of expressionism, futurism, Cubism, and other isms, the highest manifestations of artistic genius. I do not understand them. I experience no joy from them."

The broad and attractive intelligibility of the old literature also explains Lenin's partiality for the classics. Almost everybody who has published recollections of Lenin and his relation to literature has emphasized his love for the classics. When going abroad Lenin took with him, besides books on economics, the poems of Nekrassov and Goethe's Faust (recollections of Meshcheriakov). Kamenev lists the Russian classics especially loved by Lenin: Tolstoy, Pushkin, Nekrassov, Chekhov. Lepeshinsky adds to this list Shakespeare, Schiller, Byron. Lenin even had a look at Boratynsky and Tiuchev, and moreover Tiuchev who, as Bogdanov has demonstrated, so finely "organized" the psychology of the reader in a direction opposed to the goals and aspirations of the proletariat, enjoyed, according to Lepeshinsky, "his highest favor." Krupskaia speaks of Lyermontv, Pushkin and Nekrassov, whom Lenin read in moments of extreme weariness. According to Krupskaia, Lenin not only read the classics, but re-read Turgenev, Tolstoy and Chernishevsky's "What Is To Be Done?" Krupskaia remembers that it was Lenin who after the creation of the State Publishing House set them the task of issuing a cheap edition of the Russian classics. We meet the same names in the Recollections of Kryzhanovsky, Lebedev-Poliansky and Sosnovsky.

Thus there stands before us a figure of Lenin far from resembling the shut-in economist, pushing out of his way the questions of art and creative literature. It seems that Lenin was not so far away from literature and art. And this means that the remarks of this man of genius upon the questions now disturbing us have a first-class importance.

4

In the articles on Leo Tolstoy Lenin distinguishes two aspects of his creative work: 1) This artistic genius not only gave incomparable pictures of Russian life, but also

2) first-class contributions to world literature. This "but also" implies that artistic literature not only "reflects" life, but has still other properties which make these "reflections" special things capable of rising to the level of "first-class" creations of world literature. Pictures may be first-class or not first-class. Obviously then the level of the art is dependent not upon its material (portrayal, reflection) but also upon the manner of working up the material, the artistic medium, the quality of art. In an article, *L. N. Tolstoy*, written in 1910, Lenin analyzes Tolstoy's creations. "Tolstoy, portraying for the most part the old pre-revolutionary Russia"—writes Lenin— "was able in his works to rise to such *artistic* power (italics ours) that his creations have occupied one of the highest places in the poetic literature of the world." Here again two aspects: 1) The depth of the questions, the acute grasp of the material, and 2) "artistic power," that is, a certain property possessed by the material the artist portrays. "He gave in his artistic creations such a portrayal of this manner of life as belongs to the best works of world literature"—so we read in the article *L. N. Tolstoy and the Contemporary Workers' Movement*. If we remember all that has been said above about Lenin's views of art, it becomes clear just what he meant when he spoke of the "artistry of genius" and the "extraordinary power" of Tolstoy as an artist. He meant that same accessibility to broad masses in spite of the depth with which the theme is grasped, that ability to give artistic enjoyment, that simplicity, clarity, beauty. Without these qualities there would be no great artist; there would be no artist at all. Only the presence of

definite qualities independent of the material which is put into the work makes a writer an artist—that is, a creator of works of art. This is one of the conclusions to be drawn from a study of what Lenin has said about art.

In what way are Tolstoy's works remarkable from Lenin's point of view? In that he was a magnificent mirror of the Russian revolution—that is, of a whole historic epoch.

"Tolstoy is great," wrote Lenin in the article of 1908, "as the voice of those ideas and those moods which were forming among millions of the Russian peasantry up to the beginning of the bourgeois revolution in Russia."

Let us analyze this assertion. According to Lenin, Tolstoy, "a landlord humiliating himself in the name of Christ," a noble, a representative of the exploiting class became "the voice of the moods of millions of peasants" —a thought to the background of which one could devote an extended investigation. Does it contradict Marxism? Not in the least. But it refutes the rudimentary babble to the effect that a writer's creation is *bound up* with his class origin. The social origin of the writer, taken abstractly, has in itself nothing to say as to what ideas and moods—those of his own class or another's— this writer will reflect. All depends on the concrete historic conditions in which the writer's creative life develops, and upon certain special circumstances of his personal growth. Hence it is that the aristocrat, the landlord, overcomes the spiritual inheritance of his class, even breaks with it, even takes the offensive *against* it. This process is analogous to that which made ideologists and leaders of the proletariat out of Karl Marx, the son of a lawyer, Frederick Engels, the son of a manufacturer, George Plekhanov and Vladimir Lenin, deriving from the Russian privileged castes, etc. To be sure this can not be taken as a rule. We can not draw the conclusion from this that class origin is nothing and necessitates nothing. That would be an absurd distortion of Marxism. The point is that Marx and Engels, Lenin and Plekhanov, and a lot more besides, were units, exceptions to the rule, figures who by virtue of outstanding intellectual qualities in favorable historic conditions were able to conquer within themselves the spiritual influences of their class. The general axiom of Marxism as to the influence of class upon a man's psychology, the class inheritance, remains valid. But this axiom presents in the sphere of ideological creation a series of exceptions which demand a flexible, and above all not a blind, application of the rule.

What is the significance of this "exception" in our analysis of works of art? It is very great. The bad Marxist, in approaching works of art, will try to analyze these works by a mechanical application of the "rule," ignoring the possibility of "exceptions." In other words, in the sphere of art, in the analyzing of the class character of creations and the work of individual writers, the Marxian method should be flexible, broad and deep, allowing for the most various possible divergences of the creative ideology of the artist from the interests of his native class —even up to the point of open struggle against it. But these divergences in each separate instance must in the first place be found, and in the second place their origin explained—that is, the mechanism discovered of the social influence upon the writer which brought him over from the standpoint of his class to the standpoint of alien classes. It stands to reason that such an interpretation of Marxian method destroys the rudimentary, cheap, vulgar system of "Marxist" criticism, according to which the character of an artistic creation is determined by the class origin of the artist. Here Marxism is not so much "applied" as "distorted." This axiom of Marxism which speaks of the possibility of a break between an artist and his class—a picture to be observed oftenest of all in analyzing the greatest works of art—refutes Bogdanov's construction about the organizing influence of non-proletarian art as necessarily tending in a direction contrary to the interests of the proletariat. In what direction do classical art works organize the mind of the proletariat? That can be decided in each separate case *only with the help of a concrete investigation*. To assert that all world literature written not from the collective-labor point of view "organizes" the mind of the proletarian reader in a direction contrary to his interests—this is to land in a dry and dead schematism with which nothing could be accomplished either in art or in a desert.

Lenin's analysis of Tolstoy refutes the cheap and wooden application of Marxism. Yes, Tolstoy was a landlord "humiliating himself in the name of Christ." But along with that "he was able with extraordinary power to communicate the mood of the broad masses oppressed by the exploiting order, portray their situation, express their fundamental feeling of protest and indignation." (Article of 1910.) Tolstoy was a lord and an aristocrat, he was *Count* Tolstoy; nevertheless in his creations we find "a hot passionate, often ruthlessly sharp protest against the state and the police-functionary church." We find further "an inflexible rejection of private property in land," and even "an indictment of capitalism full of the deepest feeling and of burning indignation." All this is emphasized by Lenin in the creative work of a landlord, a noble, an aristocrat. But together with these traits, which constitute the immortal in our heritage from Tolstoy, Lenin points out that this hot protestant, this passionate accuser, this great critic, "displayed at the same time such lack of understanding of the causes of the crisis, and the means of transcending the crisis advancing upon Russia, as is proper only to a patriarchal naïve peasant, not to an educated European writer." Here the dependence upon a historically undeveloped milieu, upon undeveloped economic relations, constitutes the second aspect of Tolstoy as an artist. Even a genius can not always overcome the historic conditions of his epoch. The epoch enters with its contradictions and undeveloped traits into his personal experience. And from this point Lenin paints another side of Tolstoy, his self-contradiction, his religious evangel. The artistic genius, the great writer, Tolstoy, is "as ridiculous as a prophet discovering a new panacea for the salvation of mankind." "On the one hand a ruthless criticism of capitalist exploitation, an exposure of governmental violence, of the comedy of the courts and state administration, an uncovering of the whole depth of the contradiction between the growth of riches and conquest of civilization, and the growth of destitution, of savagery and martyrdom in the toiling masses; on the other hand, this crank's evangel of 'non-resistance to evil' by violence. On the one hand, the soberest realism, the tearing off of all masks of every kind; on the other hand a preaching of one of the vilest things which is to be found on this earth, namely, religion, an attempt to set up in the place of priests on government service, priests by moral conviction—that is, a cultivation of the most refined and therefore especially contemptible priestism." "In very truth," exclaims Lenin:

> *"You are poor and you are rich,*
> *You are mighty and you are weak,*
> *Mother Russia."*

In a few brief words Lenin reveals the cause of this contradictoriness in the views and teachings of Tolstoy. "These contradictions are not accidental," he says. They are an expression of the contradictory conditions in which Russian life was placed during the last third of the 19th century. The picture of Tolstoy's spiritual transformation is explained. In the contradictions of Tolstoy, in the weak sides of his creative work, was expressed the lax and the undeveloped sides of our Russian life. Hence Tolstoy is a "mirror" not only of the power, but also of the "weakness," not only of the revolutionary surge, the protest, the hate, the indignation, but also the softness of body, the unripe dreaminess and similar qualities. His productions throw into high relief "the unique historic traits of the whole first Russian revolution—its strength and its weakness."

What should be the attitude of the Russian proletariat and the Russian peasantry to the works of Tolstoy? That Russia whose strength and weakness is expressed in his works has gone into the past and will not return. What remains from the heritage of Tolstoy to our generation of fighters?

"In the heritage of Tolstoy," Lenin answers, "there is something which has not gone into the past, which belongs to the future. The Russian proletariat takes this inheritance and works upon it." The proletariat will explain to the masses of the toiling and exploited "the significance of Tolstoy's criticism of the state, of the church, of private property in land," not in order that the masses, knowing of this, shall calm themselves, but in order that this knowledge gleaned from the writings of a great artist shall raise still higher the energy of the struggle. The creations of "a landlord humiliating himself in the name of Christ" whose teaching is "unconditionally utopian and its content reactionary in the most accurate and deepest sense of this word" (Article of 1911)—the creations of this artist Lenin fearlessly offers to the proletariat as spiritual food, not dreading that the proletariat will die of its poison, its utopianism, its reactionism, its contradictions. According to Lenin's thought the danger lies not in utopianism and reactionism themselves; the harmful thing is to *idealize* this utopianism and reactionism, to idealize the teaching of Tolstoy, to attempt to justify and mitigate it. But should not the social essence of the proletariat, its class psychology, remove the possibility of such idealization? It is for this reason that those reactionary traits of Tolstoy do not overshadow in Lenin's eyes the great artistically demonstrative value for the proletariat of his creations. It is for this reason that, having studied Tolstoy in detail and knowing through and through his affirmative and negative qualities, Lenin wrote of the necessity of making the great productions of this "landlord" the actual property of all, and declared that his artistic creations "will always be treasured and read by the masses, when they have created for themselves human conditions of life by throwing off the yoke of landlords and capitalists."

Such are the inferences which we may draw from Lenin's few small articles about Tolstoy. It is regrettable that these articles have not become accessible to the broadest masses, that little has been written about them, that many comrades who "rely" on Lenin, have not taken the trouble to examine attentively that which Lenin said about art. If all this had been done in good season and adequately, there would have been fewer crude mistakes in the literary struggle which has occupied our attention during these recent years. The correct road would have been discovered at a smaller cost. Lenin is the best leader not only in the sphere of politics and economics, but also upon questions of literature and culture. The whole trend of the struggle under the slogans "proletarian culture" and "proletarian literature" during the current decade has proceeded, not under the influence of Lenin's views of art and culture, but to a considerable degree under the influence of the views of A. A. Bogdanov. Ever since the foundation of the Proletcult, thanks to the group *At-Your-Post* the ideas of A. A. Bogdanov have taken root. This means that too little attention has been given to the views of Lenin upon those questions which Bogdanov had the luck to place upon the order of the day for our discussion. It will therefore be of interest to expound the views of Lenin not only about literature, but also about proletarian culture.

5

As upon questions of art and literature, so also about proletarian culture, Lenin never expressed himself specifically and in detail. Nevertheless we have a number of statements on this subject, beginning with the *Remarks of a Publicist* printed in 1910, and ending with his speeches at congresses and conferences, even at meetings and sessions on political education, congresses of the communist youth, and also the articles *About Cooperation, Better, Less and Better,* and in various other places. We have also a precious and most complete document testifying to the views of Lenin about the debated questions of proletarian culture—his pencilled comments on the article of V. Pletnev, *On the Ideological Front,* printed in Pravda, September 27, 1922.

Let us turn to the remarks of Lenin upon this article. It is sufficient to glance over all the underlinings, *nota bene's,* exclamations, which Lenin made upon this or that "theoretic" formula of Pletnev, in order to see his ironical and mocking attitude. However, Lenin was not laughing at Pletnev, whom as we well know he valued as a talented worker. What aroused his sarcastic irony was the immaturity of theoretic judgment, the confusion of ideas, which abound in the article of the president of the Proletcult. "The creation of a new proletarian *class* culture is the fundamental goal of the Prolet-cult," wrote Pletnev. "Ha, ha!" writes Lenin in the margin, and underlines with two pencil strokes the words "creation of a new" and "fundamental." In the next sentence—"The exposition and concentration of the creativeness of the proletarian power in the sphere of science and art is the fundamental practical task"— Lenin underlines with one stroke the words "exposition and concentration" and "is the fundamental task," and with two strokes the words "science" and "practical." And with these mere underlinings, now with one and now with two strokes, and with the four letters "Ha, ha!" Lenin exposes the utter superficiality of Pletnev's treat-ment of this immensely broad task. From his underlin-ings and ironic remarks, such as "humm!" "What a mess!" and others, his utterly adverse appraisal of the assertions of the President of the Proletcult becomes completely clear. The sentence, "The task of the creation of a proletarian culture can be fulfilled by the forces *only* (underlined by Lenin) of the proletariat itself, by scholars, artists, engineers, etc., issuing from *its* (under-lined by Lenin) midst"—this sentence evokes from Lenin the comment: *"arch-fiction."* In two places he writes: "Bunk." First, where Pletnev assures the reader that the "first steps" on the road to the creation of a new method-ology of scientific creation "must be made by the pro-letariat itself," and second, beside the phrase "the pro-letarian artist will be at the same time artist and worker."

These comments may evoke a number of bewildered

questions. It seems then—an inexperienced reader may inquire—that the leader and ideologist of the proletariat was against the building of a proletarian culture? It seems that he was a partisan of bourgeois culture? If Lenin was not with Bogdanov, does not that mean that he was with the bourgeoisie?

No, it means nothing of the kind. *Against* the theory of the Proletcult—that means *for* the actual building of a proletarian culture. For this question will not be solved by the help of that literary schematism with which Bogdanov tried to solve it, nor with the help of that shame-faced and concealed Bogdanovism with which his successor, Pletnev, made the same attempt.

For Bogdanov the creation of a "proletarian culture" was bound up with the existence of the Proletcult as an organization which set up this act of creation as its own principal task. But surely culture, in the genuine meaning of the term, is a combination of knowledge and technique in all spheres. "Culture" is not only the composing of verses and stories and the painting of pictures, not only the writing of plays and putting them on the stage; it is political creation and economic creation, scientific and artistic and technical and all other kinds of creation. The sphere of culture is many-sided just as the broad struggle for life is many-sided. And to say that the "task," the "fundamental aim of the Proletcult" is the creation of a *new* proletarian *class* culture, is to utter a laughable idea to which "ha, ha!" is the appropriate answer. Only a superficial eye, a light-minded attitude to the "new class culture," and to that which a small cultural educative organization like the Proletcult is able to do, only these qualities can explain the serious face with which the fundamental propositions of the Proletcult philosophy have been propounded. It is a joke to talk about the creation of a *new* culture in our country with a population of 150 million not even literate, lacking the elementary acquisitions of the simplest culture, a country with an overwhelming majority of peasants, still in the bonds of superstition, etc., a country where we must still work long in order to lift ourselves to the level of technical well-being upon which the bourgeois countries already stand. In the absence of roads, schools, hospitals, with inadequate working ability, with the small productivity of factory and agricultural labor, with our cultural backwardness, with the heterogeneity of the working class itself, with all these circumstances to be overcome before it is possible to make any forward move, Bogdanov, and after him Pletnev, endowed their organization with the proud task of "creating" in their studios and laboratories a "new" independent proletarian culture. Bogdanov intended to do this outside of the communist party, parallel with it. Pletnev renounced this utopian idea, assuming that it contained the whole sin and weakness of the Bogdanov construction. He assumed that it was sufficient to renounce Bogdanov's invention of an "independent" third movement of the working class alongside the party and the trade unions, in order that the tasks which this movement had set itself, utopian in their very essence, should cease to be utopian and lose their grandiosely pretentious character.

And Lenin opposed this utopian naïve conception of

the mode of creation of a "new proletarian culture" with a real and realistic attitude to this question. We have spoken above of his wonderful ability to grasp an object from the side of the "ought" and the "existent." On the side of the "ought" Lenin did not deny the importance of creating an independent proletarian culture. But he laughed at those who assumed that a proletarian culture could break with the past on principle, and turning its back upon the so-called treasures of the old culture, create out of itself in a blank space some kind of new heretofore unseen treasures. This, in the first place. And in the second place Lenin saw that the creation of a new independent proletarian culture will take place, and in reality is taking place, not in the studios and laboratories and lecture halls of the Proletcult, but there where the actual and dirty work of the struggle with backwardness, with filth and ignorance and illiteracy, with belated forms of agriculture, with drunkenness, with low productivity of labor, with lack of discipline, etc., is going on. On March 13, 1919, at a meeting in Leningrad Lenin spoke of the fact that having smashed the old state apparatus, the toilers had not yet completed their work. "You will not be content with this crushing of capitalism. You must take the whole culture which capitalism left and create socialism out of it. You must take the whole science, technique, the whole knowledge, the art. Without that we cannot create the life of the communist society. And this science, technique and art is in the hands of specialists and in their heads."

And at the third All-Russian Congress of the Communist Youth on October 4, 1920, he devoted some special words to the "talk about proletarian culture."

"Without a clear understanding that only with an accurate knowledge of the culture created by the whole development of mankind, only by working it over, can we create a proletarian culture—without this understanding we will never fulfill this task."

We see that Lenin did not deny the necessity of building a "proletarian culture," but he emphasized the fact that it could be constructed only on the basis of the experience of the whole preceding science and technique, on the foundation of the old bourgeois culture critically worked over. In the same speech Lenin pointed to the example of Marxism, which grew out of the enormous knowledge of the preceding bourgeois science, out of all that had been created before Marx by human society. Marx not only took these enormous knowledges, but "submitted them to criticism," "omitting not one single point from his attention."

"The proletarian culture is not something that jumps up from nobody knows where. It is not a thought-up scheme of some people who call themselves specialists in proletarian culture. That is all pure nonsense. The proletarian culture must appear as a natural development of those stores of knowledge which man has worked out under the yoke of the capitalist society, the landlord society, the bureaucratic society.

"All these roads and little paths have led, and are leading, and will continue to lead, to the proletarian culture, just as the political economy remodeled by Marx showed us to what human society must come, pointed out the transition to working-class struggle, to the beginning of the proletarian revolution."

It is sufficient to compare these brief words with what has been said about "an independent class proletarian culture," and about "bourgeois culture," in order to see how clear is the Leninist approach to this question.

"While we were jabbering about proletarian culture" —wrote Lenin in January, 1923, in his *Page from a Diary* —"and about its relation with the bourgeois culture, facts have been presented to us and figures demonstrating that even in the matter of bourgeois culture things with us are weak indeed. It became known that, as we might have expected, we are still far behind the goal of universal literacy, and even our progress in comparison with tzarist times (1897) has been too slow. This will serve as a warning threat and rebuke to those who have been soaring and are soaring in the empyrean of 'proletarian culture.' That shows how much real dirty work remains for us to do in order to attain the level of an ordinary civilized state of western Europe. It shows, moreover, what a mountain of work stands before us now before we can attain, on the basis of our proletarian acquisitions, any kind of real cultural level at all."

To the talk about proletarian culture Lenin opposed a genuine creation of it, but conceived it not as an invention of "theories" about culture, not as a teaching of theatrical art to young proletarians and peasants, or the art of writing verse, or the art of painting pictures. The creation of a proletarian culture was conceived by Lenin in the broad practical sense as the propagation of literacy, the betterment of the life conditions in which the masses live, the elevation of the technique of agriculture and industry, improvement of the methods of work, increasing of technical and every other kind of qualification, the acquisition over and above literacy of the existing scientific education—the lowest, the minimum, the high, the specialized and the general—a critical appropriation and remodelling of the existing treasures of art and culture, a creation of things which will change for the better the common conditions of existence, the extermination of ignorance, superstition, crude—in a word, as the broadest possible movement into which we must draw the popular masses in every corner of our enormous country. In the face of the scientific and technical successes of contemporary bourgeois civilization our backwardness did indeed seem appalling. And in the face of this appalling backwardness it must indeed have seemed worthy of cruel mockery, that lofty-souled chatter about laboratory creation, about a new independent class culture, while every day at every step we were stumbling upon the crying gaps in our uncultivated life. And Yakovlev was quite right, and in full agreement with what we know from other statements of Lenin about literature and art, in his formulation of the fundamental disagreement between the point of view of a genuinely proletarian culture, a culture proletarian in creativeness, and the point of view of a culture "proletarian" in quotation marks, or rather a "Proletcultish culture."

"1) Not only the isolated Proletcult detachment, but the whole proletariat is confronted with a struggle for culture, in which the peasant masses will advance together with the proletariat.

"2) Not a dilettant, self-admiring, Proletcultish so-called science, not a lot of chatter about 'socialization' which not one worker will understand, but a serious education, lasting for many and many years, of new and ever new hundreds of thousands of workers and peasants."

In his famous article *On Cooperation* Lenin wrote:

"To tell the truth we have '*only*' [the italics and quotation marks are characteristic] one thing to do: to make our population so 'civilized' that it will understand all the advantages of participating to the last man in cooperation, and will organize that participation. 'Only' this. No other ingenuities are necessary for us now in order to make the transition to socialism. But for this, in order to achieve this 'only,' a whole revolution is necessary, a whole period of cultural development of the entire popular mass.

"Our enemies have told us more than once that we are undertaking an unreasonable task of planting socialism in an inadequately cultured country. But they misunderstand the fact that we began not at that end which was postulated in the theories of all sorts of pedants, but that with us the political and social revolution turned out to be a predecessor of the *cultural revolution, that cultural revolution before which we nevertheless now stand.*

"For us that cultural revolution is now enough to make us a completely socialist country, but for us that cultural revolution presents unbelievable difficulties both of a purely cultural character (for we are illiterate) and of a material character, for in order to have culture a certain development of the material forces of production, a certain material basis, is necessary."

"The cultural revolution"—that is, a long period of ceaseless labor in all spheres, from the alphabet to astronomical calculation, from building baths to aerial navigation, from trade schools to academies of invention, from the liquidation of backward forms of agriculture to the building of artificial fertilizer factories. From top to bottom in all spheres, the lowest and the highest, a tireless uninterrupted work must go on, not only in the cultural institutions, schools, universities, libraries and factories, but throughout the whole country, in the backwoods corners, in every hut, in the workshop, in every worker's chamber, otherwise the work will be unsuccessful. For only on condition of its collective character, only on condition that the majority joins in with the working class in the lead—only such work can receive the proud name of that cultural revolution through which we must make our way to socialism.

And again we ask the reader: If we compare those discourses about an "independent class proletarian culture," which we have heard from Bogdanov and other partisans of the Proletcult, with these thoughts which Lenin has left us, fragmentary and on various themes, do we not see a gulf between them, and do we not see the whole truth and rightness, real and deep, able at the same time to show the ultimate goal and the concrete roads through which, not quickly, not at once, and at the price of enormous efforts, but nevertheless in the long run surely, we shall make our way!

Lenin's reflections about proletarian culture decide also the question whether Lenin was with the *At-Your-Post* group as Comrade Vardin asserted, or against them. And indeed V. Pletnev, too, before the publication of his article in Pravda with Lenin's notations, covered himself with the authority of our late leader. There can be no doubt about it. Lenin and his teaching—Leninism— were against the *At-Your-Post* group. In the teaching of this group there was more Bogdanovism than Leninism. The *At-Your-Post* group are the illegitimate children of A. A. Bogdanov.

6

Here it is necessary to touch upon the article of Lenin, *Party Organization and Party Literature.*

In order to understand this or that statement of Lenin made in the past, whether remote or near, it is necessary to have a clear idea of the concrete historical situation in which the statement was made. This is an axiom of dialectic materialism.

And what was the moment when this article was written? It was November, 1905. Our party had for the first time come out of the underground. It was confronted with the task of gathering the genuine revolutionary forces, the struggle against all kinds of non-partyism, against the old methods of legal Marxism. Lenin, indeed, in the first line of the article speaks of the "new conditions for social democratic work [in that epoch our party was called social democratic] created in Russia after the October revolution." These new conditions evoked the problem of *party* literature. Up to 1905 the entire legal social democratic activity was non-party. That is, it did not enter into the party organization, but stood outside. That is to say that in the organizational sense it was independent, a fact which reflected itself, of course, in its activity by a divergence from the revolutionary path. In this Lenin was talking only of the "social democratic literature," and not of the Social Revolutionary which at that time was also both legal and illegal. The legal social democratic press, formally non-party, could consequently side by side with the party illegal literature, steer its own course upon questions upon which a united will was demanded. And Lenin objected to the fact that a literature considering itself "party," that is, a social democratic literature, might remain *outside* of the party organization, might remain non-party. The new situation produced by the successes of the revolution of 1905 demanded, although with large exceptions, a change in the conditions of existence of the social democratic press.

"Whether we will or no," wrote Lenin, "the situation of the revolution compels us to undertake immediately a new organization of affairs. Literature can now even 'legally' be nine-tenths party. Literature ought to become party."

"Down with the non-party *littérateurs!*" exclaimed Lenin. "Down with the superman *littérateurs!* The liter-

ary work ought to become a *part* of the general proletarian work, a 'cog' or 'screw' of the one great social
democratic mechanism, put in motion by the whole conscious vanguard of the entire working class. The literary
work ought to become a constituent part of the organized,
planned, united social democratic party work."

Lenin emphasizes the fact that he is talking about "the
literary part of the *party* work of the proletariat." In
answer to objections which might be offered he puts
forward the thought that in fact even this part "cannot
be mechanically identified with the other parts of the
party work of the proletariat." And further on Lenin
makes clear those elements of which the literary business
consists, which having been formerly "non-party" he
considers it necessary to bring into the party:

"The newspapers ought to enter immediately into the
party organizations. The printing plants and store houses,
magazines and reading rooms, libraries and various book-
stands—all this ought to become party and accountable
to the party." It goes without saying that the journals
which were carrying on the work of the party, in which
both party and non-party writer-artists had been able to
publish their writings, ought to become party journals.

And foreseeing the objection: "Do you mean to say
you would submit to the collectivity such a delicate individual thing as literary creation, etc.?" Lenin answered
his imagined objectors:

"Rest easy, gentlemen. In the first place *I am talking
about party literature and its subjection to party control!*" And in supplementation of this limiting remark
he added his sarcastically penetrating and just comments

upon the so-called "freedom" of creation in bourgeois society.

Concluding his article Lenin again formulates his position:

"The whole social democratic literature ought to become party. All newspapers, journals, printing plants, etc. ought to undertake the work of reorganization immediately" etc. It is a question of social democratic literature, and Lenin's thought, always crystal clear and precise, is clear in this case, too. It is a question of converting into "party" that *social democratic* literature which being legal had been carrying on the work of the party without belonging to it.

Lenin rarely contradicted himself, especially if you take into consideration in each case the different periods of time. And if you wish to know how Lenin looked upon artistic creation, you will find in this article written in 1905 and in the memoirs of Clara Zetkin, all her conversations with Lenin carried on after 1917—that is, more than twelve years later—almost the same thought about "creative freedom" expressed in almost the same words.

"Everyone is free to write and say everything he wants to without the slightest limitation," wrote Lenin in 1905 in that same article. But he added "Every free union (including the party) is also free to expel such members as use the party name for the propagation of anti-party views." Lenin recognized the "freedom" of the political writer to write whatever he wants to (the writer remembering, however, that if his "free" creation goes against the views of the party he will simply be thrown out of it). So much the more did he grant such "creative freedom" to the artist. And indeed in his conversations with Clara Zetkin Lenin spoke of the very fact that our revolution "had freed the artist from the yoke" under which art had existed in the bourgeois structure, with its complete dependence upon the whims and caprices of the tzarist court and the aristocrats and the bourgeoisie. "Every artist, every one who considers himself such, has the right to create freely according to his own ideal, independently of everything." So Comrade Zetkin quotes us Lenin's words. "Of course," he added, "we are communists, we ought not to fold our hands and let chaos develop whither it will. We ought in a thoroughly planful manner to guide this process and mould its results." We ought to lead, we ought to recognize the creative freedom of every artist, taking into consideration the concrete peculiarities of this part of the literary work, and not shutting our eyes to all its variety and complexity.

NOTES AND REFERENCES

Page 4—Selvinsky's poem was quoted in *Les Nouvelles Litteraires,* Paris, August 8, 1931.

The statement of Tretiakov is from *Literatura Facta* (The Literature of Fact), Moscow, 1929, pp. 266–7. "Gublit" and "Glavlit" are abbreviations, respectively, for Provincial and Central Department of Literary Affairs.

Page 5—Trotsky: Vol. I, Chapter I, of his *History of the Russian Revolution.*

Page 7—The report of the Kharkov Congress, and all the English publications of the International Union of Revolutionary Writers, are distributed by the International Publishers, New York.

Page 12—My comment is particularly directed to Trotsky's article, *Socialism in a Separate Country,* printed as Appendix Two in Vol. III of his *History of the Russian Revolution.*

Page 19—The report of the delegates to the Kharkov Congress was printed in *The New Masses* for February, 1931.

Page 20—"Filial": Walt Carmon in the *Literaturnaia Gazeta* (Moscow) October 14, 1930. "We look upon ourselves as a filial bureau."

Page 21—The quotation is from *International Literature,* Nos. 2–3, 1932.

Page 22—The report appeared in *The New Masses* for September, 1932.

Page 29—E. E. Cummings: *Eimi*, p. 34.

Page 36—*Pravda:* Issue of May 14, 1932.
Engels: Preface to the second edition of *Anti-Dühring.*

Page 37—Trotsky: *Literature and Revolution,* English translation, pp. 178 and 218.
Lenin: Letter of February 25, 1908.

Page 41—"A literature . . .": Quoted from Lelevich, one of the leaders of the At-Your-Postites, by V. Sayanov in his *Contemporary Literary Groupings* (Leningrad, 1930). I am much indebted to this book for general information presented from the point-of-view of the bureaucracy. My chief debt for information from the point-of-view of creative intelligence is to Polonsky's *Outline of the Literary Movement of the Revolutionary Epoch* (Moscow, 1928).

Page 42—The quotation is from Sianov, loc. cit. p. 109–10.

Page 43—Engels' letter is in *Karl Marx—Friedrich Engels, Briefe an A. Bebel, W. Liebknecht, K. Kautsky und Andere* (Moscow–Leningrad, 1933).

Page 44—The verses are quoted by Sianov, loc. cit. p. 114, from Byezimensky.

Page 48—Nicolas Seeland: Cited by Roback in his *Psychology of Character,* pp. 70–72.

Page 52—Trotsky: In *Yessenin, Life, Personality, Creations,* a memorial collection (Moscow, 1925) p. 93 ff.

Page 53—The quotations are from Karl Marx, *Communist Manifesto* and *Theses on Feuerbach.*

Page 56—Voronsky: *Krassnaia Nov,* 1926, Book 2.

Page 61—Voronsky: *About Art,* p. 59.
Kirillov: Quoted in *The Literary Gazette.*

Page 63—Maiakovsky: *How Poems Are Made* (1931). Other selections from this work appeared in English in a recent number of *The Living Age.*

Page 71—Maiakovsky died April 14, 1930.

Page 72—The party paper: *Pravda,* April 15, 1930.
Trotsky: *Bulletin of the Left Opposition,* May, 1930.
The memorial article in *Literaturnaia Gazeta* (April 11, 1932) is by Selivanovsky.

Page 76—The quotations from the Serapions are given by Sianov, loc. cit. p. 65 ff.

Page 77—Trotsky: *Literature and Revolution,* pp. 70 and 75.

Page 79—The quotations are from speeches of Auerbach and Rodov at the Conference of the Literary Department of the Central Committee of the Russian Communist Party, May 9, 1924 (published in a pamphlet by *Krassnaia Nov,* 1924).

Page 80—Vsevolod Ivanov: *The Literary Gazette,* December 23, 1929.
Tikhonov and Slonimsky: Ibid, September 24, 1930.

Page 83—Zamyatin: From his contribution to the collection, *Artists About Art and About Themselves.*

Page 84—Zamyatin: Quoted in the English translator's introduction to his novel.

Page 86—*The Literary Gazette:* August 26, 1929.

Page 96—Trotsky: *Bulletin of the Left Opposition,* No. 28.

Page 98—*The Literary Gazette:* June 15, 1931.

Page 99—Romanov's letter is in *The Literary Gazette* of July 15, 1931.

Page 104—Ella Winter: *Red Virtue.*

Page 111—*The Literary Gazette:* August 26, 1929.

Page 113—Pilnyak's letter is in *The Literary Gazette* for September 2, 1929.

Page 120—*The Literary Gazette:* September 9, 1929.

Page 124—Michael Gold: *The New Masses,* October, 1931.

Page 126—*The Literary Gazette:* December 19, 1930.

Page 127—Pereversev: See the article by L. Auerbach in *Na Lit. Postu,* 1930, No. 1.

Page 128—Gorbachev: *The Literary Gazette,* May 26, 1930.

Page 129—*Literature and Revolution:* p. 218.

Page 135—Diego Rivera: *What Is Art For?, The Modern Monthly,* June, 1933.

Page 136—Trotsky: *Literature and Revolution,* p. 205. Lenin: See p. 243 ff. of this book.

Page 139—The speeches made at the conference were published by *Krassnaia Nov,* Moscow, 1924, in the pamphlet entitled: *On the Question of the Policy of the Russian Communist Party in Artistic Literature.*

Page 142—*The Literary Gazette:* Editorial of May 17, 1932.

NOTES AND REFERENCES

Page 147—Freeman: *Voices of October*, p. 54. Polonsky: *Outline of the Literary Movement of the Revolutionary Epoch*, p. 278.

Page 149—Voronsky: My quotations are from *About Art* and *The Art of Seeing the World.*

Page 158—Lenin: *Complete Works*, Vol. XXIX, p. 40.

Page 159—The article of Louis Fischer, *A Revolution in Revolutionary History*, appeared in *The New York Herald-Tribune*, November 27, 1932.

Page 164—*Na Lit. Postu:* December, 1929.

Page 166—*Literary Gazette*, December 23, 1929.

Page 168—"So far from constituting a revolution": Even the verbal form of the decree abolishing RAPP, which is far from explaining it, makes plain that no fundamental change in the theory or practice of "literary politics" is intended. The motivation of the decree reads as follows:

"At the present time, when the *cadres* of proletarian literature and art have had time to grow up, when new writers and artists have arisen from the factories, mills and collective farms, the framework of the existing proletarian literary and artistic organizations (All-Union Association of Proletarian Writers, Russian Association of Proletarian Writers, Russian Association of Proletarian Musicians, etc.) is proving to be too narrow and to act as a serious hindrance to the full development of creative work in art. This gives rise to the danger that these organizations will be converted from instruments for mobilizing to the utmost the Soviet writers and artists around the tasks of socialist construction into a means of cultivating group exclusiveness, isolation from the political tasks of the present moment and from the large groups of writers and artists who sympathize with socialist construction."

Pravda: May 14, 1932.

Auerbach's four-hour speech was made at a "Poetic Conference of RAPP" on the night of April 17th. Mr. Fischer reports another speech on the day before his organization was dissolved.

Page 169—"The next issue of *The Literary Gazette*": May 17th.

Page 178—Aristotle: *Metaphysics,* 1004b 25.
Abelard: Quoted by Henry Osborn Taylor in the *Mediaeval Mind,* Vol. II, p. 379.

Page 184—Marx: *Zur Kritik der Hegelschen Rechtsphilosophie,* in *Aus dem Literarischen Nachlass,* p. 385.

Page 185—The denunciation of Hegel is in *Die Heilige Familie* and the renunciation of philosophy in general in favor of empirical science in *Die Deutsche Ideologie, Marx-Engels Archiv,* Vol. I, pp. 237 and 240.

Page 186—Engels: *Ludwig Feuerbach,* Sec. 1.
Marx: *The Civil War in France,* Sec. III. The word "noble" I borrow from Charles Longuet's French translation of the word "higher" in the same passage.

Page 187—Marx: *Die Heilige Familie,* Chap. IV.

Page 188—Benedetto Croce: *What Is Living and What Is Dead of the Philosophy of Hegel.*

Page 189—Lenin: His notes made when studying philosophy are to be found in Vols. IX and XII of the *Leninsky Sbornik* (Lenin Collection). My quotations are from Vol. IX, p. 69, and Vol. XII, pp. 323-4-5.

Page 191—Hegel: *Logic,* p. 41.
Engels: *Anti-Dühring,* the chapter on *Dialectic.* See also my *Marx and Lenin,* p. 109.

Page 192—Feuerbach: *Grundsätze der Philosophie der Zukunft.*

"As Lange says": The Russian Marxist, Plekhanov, not interested in Feuerbach's mind, but concerned only to establish the perfect truth of dialectic materialism, exclaims against this judgment of Lange's. Plekhanov insists, even against Feuerbach himself, who expressly disclaimed the title of materialist, that his philosophy was perfectly materialistic. "Feuerbach never denied," he cries, "that the nature of man 'is only a special case in the chain of the physical processes of life.'" And that is true—he never denied it. He merely permitted his feelings to forget it—or, as Lange so carefully suggests, "inclined to turn his gaze" in a different direction. To assert, as Plekhanov does, that this proposition about the nature of man "lies at the basis of his whole philosophy", in the face of such statements as that "Truth is the totality of human life and being," "Only that is which is an object of passion," "Not to love and not to be are identical," "Where there is no sense there is no being, no real object"—to make that assertion and leave these statements unexplained and unalluded to, is to confess, it seems to me, that you are not engaged in a study of the man's mind, but in a piece of special pleading.

Page 193—Marx: *Theses on Feuerbach.*

Page 195—Engels: Letter to Joseph Block, September 21, 1890.

Marx: *The Eighteenth Brumaire of Louis Bonaparte,* p. 9; a letter to Amenkov, 1846, and a letter to Weydemeyer, 1852.

Page 201—"Bringing the proletariat a consciousness of its own destiny": This idea was first formulated by Marx in the correspondence published in the *Deutsch-Französische Jahrbücher* in 1843. "We will not then oppose the world like doctrinaires with a new principle. . . . We expose new prin-

ciples to the world out of the principles of the world itself.
. . . We explain to it only the real object for which it strug-
gles, and consciousness is a thing it must acquire even though
it objects to it."

"Lenin overstepped": I have presented these passages, and
also described some of the attacks made upon them, in the
chapter on Bolshevism in my book, *Marx and Lenin*.

Page 203—Henry Hazlitt: *Literature and the Class War*, in
The Nation for July 15, 1931, republished in his *Anatomy of
Criticism*.

Page 207—Marx: *Theses on Feuerbach*.
Trotsky: *Literature and Revolution*, p. 220.

Page 208—This explanation of the dialectic philosophy
also explains what that ritual pronouncement dictated by the
Russian "lito-politicians" to the Kharkov Congress meant:
"The method of creative art is the method of dialectic materialism." (See p. 15 ff.) It meant that every revolutionary
artist must believe that he inhabits a world whose essence is
an evolution by self-contradiction "from the lower to the
higher," and particularly a social world whose essence is such
evolution by class conflict. In such a world no serious artist
can fail to be a propagandist. If his art is realistic, it will
"show up the . . . essential driving factors," and these are
the factors of successful class struggle toward socialism. If
his art is romantic and disposed to dream, it will find but
one "essential" thing to romanticize and but one dream to
dream—the progress of the class struggle and that dream of
the classless society "which has not a vestige of illusion or
utopia." And if, notwithstanding the essential non-existence
of the individual, the artist must have a personal hero to
idealize, what heroes are there in such a world but those who
represent and guide "the essential driving factors," the leaders of the party work? Thus while we may agree that the
slogan of "dialectic" art-creation "says very little" to the aver-

age mortal, we must add that what it does say differs not one iota from the slogans, Socialist Realism, Red Romanticism, and Idealization of the Leaders. What they all say is: *The work of artists who call themselves proletarian and join this association, no matter what their school or tendency, must be communist propaganda and nothing else.* The annulment of the metaphysical formula and its replacement by these simpler slogans was not a theoretic change, nor even a change of policy in Moscow toward creative art. It was a change of diplomacy. The plan is to propagate the understanding of essences more gradually and with a certain mercy toward the limitations of the unillumined. They have, in short, withdrawn the esoteric doctrine into a narrower circle of initiates, and are feeding out to the international multitude certain more vulgarly intelligible phrases which adumbrate sufficiently for practical purposes that inviolable truth of the universe which is in Moscow and in their keeping.

Page 209—My book: *Marx and Lenin: the Science of Revolution.*

Page 210—Lenin: Draft of a resolution for the first all-Russian Congress of Proletcults, 1920. Quoted by Sianov, loc. cit. p. 107.

Page 212—Jennings: I quote the title of his book popularizing the findings of biology in this field.
The quotations from Marx are to be found in the *Theses on Feuerbach* and *The Civil War in France*, Sec. III, the quotation from Engels in his *Ludwig Feuerbach*, Sec. 1.

Page 213—Trotsky: *Literature and Revolution*, p. 230.
Oscar Wilde: *The Soul of Man under Socialism*, p. 3.

Page 214—Matthew Josephson: *Transition*, No. 14, p. 60.

INDEX

INDEX

INDEX

INDEX

INDEX